Building Asia's Security

Nick Bisley

T0386170

Building Asia's Security

Nick Bisley

IISS The International Institute for Strategic Studies

The International Institute for Strategic Studies

Arundel House I 13–15 Arundel Street I Temple Place I London I WC2R 3DX I UK

First published December 2009 by **Routledge**
4 Park Square, Milton Park, Abingdon, Oxon, OX14 4RN

for **The International Institute for Strategic Studies**
Arundel House, 13–15 Arundel Street, Temple Place, London, WC2R 3DX, UK
www.iiss.org

Simultaneously published in the USA and Canada by **Routledge**
711 Third Ave., New York, NY 10017

Routledge is an imprint of Taylor & Francis, an Informa Business

© 2009 The International Institute for Strategic Studies

DIRECTOR-GENERAL AND CHIEF EXECUTIVE John Chipman
EDITOR Tim Huxley
MANAGER FOR EDITORIAL SERVICES Ayse Abdullah
ASSISTANT EDITOR Sarah Johnstone
COVER/PRODUCTION John Buck

The International Institute for Strategic Studies is an independent centre for research, information and debate on the problems of conflict, however caused, that have, or potentially have, an important military content. The Council and Staff of the Institute are international and its membership is drawn from almost 100 countries. The Institute is independent and it alone decides what activities to conduct. It owes no allegiance to any government, any group of governments or any political or other organisation. The IISS stresses rigorous research with a forward-looking policy orientation and places particular emphasis on bringing new perspectives to the strategic debate.

The Institute's publications are designed to meet the needs of a wider audience than its own membership and are available on subscription, by mail order and in good bookshops. Further details at www.iiss.org.

British Library Cataloguing in Publication Data
A catalogue record for this book is available from the British Library

Library of Congress Cataloging in Publication Data

ISBN 978-0-415-58266-7
ISSN 0567-932X

ADELPHI 408

Contents

ACKNOWLEDGEMENTS

Several of the arguments set out in this Adelphi were first presented at the IISS–ISEAS International Expert Workshop entitled *ASEAN, Asia-Pacific Multilateralism and the Evolving Regional Security Architecture*, Singapore, October, 2009; the 7th IISS *Global Strategic Review*, Geneva, September 2009; and the *AUS–CSCAP Regional Security Issues Forum*, Melbourne, September 2008. I would like to thank the participants at those forums for their valuable insights, and to thank Gerhard Hoffstaedter for his helpful research assistance. I would also like to express my appreciation to the many people who have been very generous with their time and ideas while I researched and wrote this book. I am particularly grateful to Dan Flitton, Allan Gyngell, Malcolm Cook, Evelyn Goh, Bill Tow, Ken Jimbo, Joe Camilleri, Rob Ayson and Brendan Taylor. Most importantly, I would like to thank Tim Huxley, the Adelphi series editor, both for commissioning this research and for his outstanding editorial zeal during the production process.

NB
Melbourne,
December 2009

How do you make the Asia-Pacific century truly pacific? That was a question posed by Australian Prime Minister Kevin Rudd at a Sydney conference in December 2009 debating the possibility of a formal Asia-Pacific Community.[1] Before the summit, while promoting a revamped model of regional organisation, the PM's special envoy Richard Woolcott stressed the major shift in economic, political and strategic weight under way, moving from the Atlantic towards the Pacific.[2] Rudd himself referred to a widely held view[3] when he said Asia would be 'the absolute epicentre of global affairs in the twenty-first century'.[4]

Since the 1960s and 1970s, when a turbulent Southeast Asia was often characterised as 'the Balkans of the East', the wider Asia-Pacific region has enjoyed decades of peace, stability and – despite the setbacks of the 1997/98 financial crisis – a dramatic improvement in prosperity. However, contemporary Asia is home to several great powers, including the emerging giants of China and India. It includes North Korea, which has repeatedly defied the international community over its nuclear programme, particularly by conducting underground nuclear tests in 2006 and 2009. Territorial disputes remain unresolved between China and Japan in the South China Sea, and between the nuclear powers of India and Pakistan in the Himalayan foothills of Kashmir. China claims sovereignty over Taiwan and does not accept the province of Arunachal Pradesh as indisputably part of India.[5] In April 2009, Thai and Cambodian forces again exchanged fire near the Preah Vihear temple in the latest instalment of those two countries' long-running border dispute.[6]

There was an element of comedy to an incident off Hainan Island the previous month, when members of the Chinese navy stripped to their underwear after personnel aboard the USS *Impeccable* turned fire hoses on them.[7] However, the serious diplomatic row surrounding the *Impeccable*'s alleged surveillance of Chinese submarine activity near Hainan was a possible foretaste of future strategic competition between the United States and China.

The US, long the major power keeping the peace through its alliance system, is subtly transforming its regional strategic role. Meanwhile, defence spending across Asia is rising, as key powers expand and modernise their military capabilities.[8] Layered across the top of this, a wide array of non-traditional threats, such as terrorism, piracy, transnational criminal networks and infectious diseases, all add to the regional sense of insecurity.

Several decades of growing democracy and political pluralism in Asia have created a seemingly stable and prosperous environment. However beneath this surface lie old national rivalries and new strategic uncertainty. Full-blown warfare is still plausible. While many policymakers and analysts remain unconvinced by the prospect of a monolithic Asia-Pacific Community,[9] most agree that this increasingly important region needs better international mechanisms, including its security arrangements. It needs to improve on the institutional setting or fractured 'architecture' that currently exists if it is to deal with the clashes of interest that will inevitably arise, and other future challenges.

The speed with which regional efforts to promote security cooperation have emerged and proliferated has created a distinctly messy institutional setting. In the past 15 years, Asia has moved from having almost no regional institutions seeking explicitly to advance common security goals to a complex array of groups covering a wide spectrum of activities – from bodies that promote a sense of regional confidence to formal commitments to operate joint military patrols.

For decades there was reluctance to embrace multilateral forms of security cooperation. The US military presence was organised around bilateral arrangements, and after the ill-fated experiment of South East Asia Treaty Organisation (SEATO)[10] most states showed little interest in multilateral endeavours. Asia's nonaligned developing states were focused inwards, both in their socio-economic development priorities and their security concerns, while their geography, divergent capabilities and vastly uneven resources meant that the more affluent Western-oriented states opted for bilateral approaches.[11]

Even in the late 1980s, Asian states were uneasy about quite mild forms of multilateral security cooperation. For example, during the formation of the Asia Pacific Economic Cooperation (APEC) forum, many countries insisted that security matters were to be kept firmly off the agenda.

But pressure to counter transnational terrorism, Asia's changing strategic landscape and other issues are expediting a multilateral approach to security. Today, specifically security-focused groups exist, including the ASEAN Regional Forum (ARF), the Shanghai Cooperation Organisation (SCO) and the Trilateral Strategic Dialogue (TSD). Security is now also discussed at APEC and ASEAN Plus Three (APT) meetings.

But while states have been publicly enthusiastic about security cooperation, the substance of such cooperation has been limited. Most states continue with traditional defence and security policies; and the US alliance system – a series of bilateral military relationships with key regional powers – remains the most significant feature of the region's security setting. For the time being at least, it continues to be the central stabilising factor in the region. Moreover, while Asia's changing strategic landscape is encouraging many countries to explore collaborative efforts, it is also prompting more traditional responses. For example, the US alliance system has been strengthened and retooled since 2001, most particularly by Australia and Japan. Many states have significantly increased their defence budgets.

Historically, moments of power transition are prone to instability and the current mood in the fast-changing Asian region reflects this. Countries are not necessarily frightened by the prospect of change in Asia's shifting strategic landscape, but they are uncertain about what the future holds and are taking what they feel are prudent steps to guard against unpalatable prospects. This in turn is prompting a sense of insecurity among other countries, which then feel the need to act to protect themselves, creating a potential spiral of uncertainty and fear. It is precisely this cycle of insecurity that supporters of multilateral and cooperative approaches seek to prevent. Yet, it is still challenging to convince states that cooperation can help assuage their security concerns.

It is clear that the pattern of regional security established after the normalisation of US relations with China in the late 1970s – which was only briefly interrupted by a period of strategic drift in the early 1990s – is not going to provide the certainties of old. Changing geopolitical and economic circumstances, new technologies, shifting attitudes within Asian states and societies, as well as adjustments to America's strategic priorities and capabilities, mean that the broader structure of Asia's regional order is going to change. For its supporters, a security architecture comprised of multilateral mechanisms has an important part to play in this changing order. The wide interest in multilateral security cooperation of Asian states seems to support this basic proposition. However, precisely what the role of this security architecture will be is unclear.

The current alphabet soup of groupings, with often overlapping membership and areas of competence, has failed thus far to meet the obvious demand for more institutionalised security cooperation.[12] One reason why existing Asian security institutions have, at best, a minor impact on member states' policies is an inability to create appropriate institutions as well as the problems of replication and redundancy that have come from uncoordinated institutional proliferation.

However, some analysts feel that the shortcomings reflect more than bad institutional design or ineffective diplomacy. They believe that Asia's clashes of interests, its rivalries and the historically rooted antagonism of so many key states make substantive security cooperation of an overarching kind impossible. If this interpretation were correct, efforts to go further than building confidence among Asian states or tinkering at the margins of security policy would always be fraught.

This book takes a different view. It argues that the wide array of cooperative mechanisms that are presently part of the region's messy security architecture make a clear, if limited, contribution to regional stability. However, their potential to do more is constrained. Therefore, expanding their influence will require some important changes from policymakers and politicians in the region.

Circumstances in Asia will prevent the creation at any time in the foreseeable future of a security architecture akin to that which prevails in Europe. However, it is possible to imagine a distinctly Asian architecture, one that integrates both traditional elements, such as the American security guarantee, with well-designed, sufficiently resourced cooperative mechanisms. It could reduce the tensions caused by incipient great-power strategic rivalry, damp down the spirals of insecurity that the present power transition is creating, and foster an improved capability to respond to non-traditional security threats.

For this to come about, Asian countries will need to change their attitudes towards cooperation. At present, the growing number of regional security mechanisms masks the extent to which states feel wary of their neighbours and uncertain about their geopolitical future. There is a pressing need to develop an architecture in the coming years. Without the assurances it could provide, and the trust it could promote, there is a very real risk that the current uncertainties could breed a much more dangerous regional order.

Rather than constantly harking back to a European ideal against which the region does and will always fall short, we need to understand an Asian security architecture as being composed of different elements, such as dialogue forums, alliances and joint action interacting in a purposive fashion to promote a more stable regional order. The following chapters analyse the key components of the current fractured system, how they interact, and the broader implications for peace and prosperity in the world's most dynamic region. While the cooperative elements of the partial architecture do not contribute significantly to regional security, they do play a key part in some areas. Their absence would make the region a notably less secure place.

It is possible to glean from present modes of cooperation some indication of how an Asian security architecture might emerge. Australia has taken the lead in calling for an

Asia-Pacific Community by 2020. The recently elected Japanese prime minister, Yukio Hatoyama, has added his voice with a proposal for an East Asian Community.[13] While neither is an immediate prospect, and even their medium-term chances are limited, it is clear that a regional security architecture is needed to underwrite regional order and help Asia's states and societies maximise their human potential. Those who wish to enhance the region's security will need to focus on three central elements: the bilateral relationships of the major powers, America's bilateral alliance system and the range of cooperative multilateral security mechanisms. The challenge lies not only in getting the institutional design for security multilateralism right, but in managing a productive interaction of these three key elements.

CHAPTER ONE

Security Architecture, the Asian Way

Since the early 1990s, Asian security cooperation has increased dramatically. Almost every time the region has experienced a crisis or even a minor geopolitical shift, policymakers and analysts seem to have called for greater cooperation to deal with the exigency. The 9/11 terrorist attacks, followed by the Bali bombings of October 2002, prompted the Asia Pacific Economic Cooperation (APEC) forum to begin to talk about security and trade at the 2002 Los Cabos summit. Concerns about border stability in Central Asia led to the 2001 founding of the Shanghai Cooperation Organisation (SCO). The Trilateral Strategic Dialogue (TSD) between Australia, Japan and the United States was created in 2006 to help manage the way America's Asian alliances were being reconfigured to give allies greater autonomy locally and improve their integration into America's global strategy.

The sheer number of cooperative measures partly derives from the fact that the term is used for a diverse range of policy options. 'Security cooperation' covers everything from large-scale and high-cost alliances to low-key and commitment-free discussions. This inclusiveness can have some diplomatic and political utility. States can give the appearance of undertaking action when really the policy substance to which they have committed may be rather meagre. Equally, analysts may see more substance in such cooperation than really exists.

This makes it a complex task to determine the consequences of regional security cooperation. Just because Asian states are talking to one another with some regularity over security matters, it does not necessarily follow that the region is more stable or its societies more secure. What weight should be given to a dialogue forum? To what extent does the process of security cooperation – as opposed to its substance – generate regional benefits? Over what time frame can we expect the different types of security collaboration to deliver? It is important to clarify what 'security cooperation' means to better understand the implications of the different forms of cooperation, from bilateral dialogues through to the compelling but elusive idea of a security architecture.

Security cooperation: meaning and forms

At one level, security cooperation is just a specific form of international cooperation. Just as states share information about macroeconomic policy or commit themselves to common trade rules, they may share intelligence or make mutual defence commitments. However, the very nature of security policy – its concern with state survival and fundamental state interests – makes it a different policy sphere from most others. Cooperating on security is not the same as a trade agreement or a currency-swap arrangement because of the existential character of the interests concerned and the far greater political sensitivities surrounding them. To understand what security cooperation is requires a more specific conceptualisation.

Some have thus argued that it refers to policy coordination intended to avoid specific security outcomes, such as an arms race or nuclear proliferation.[1] Others argue that it involves agreement among a group of states, whether tacit or explicit, to restrain aspects of their mutual security policies. Yet neither of these definitions captures much of what goes on in Asian security cooperation. In many cases, one can observe countries undertaking joint activities that have no functional end and are never likely to. Yet the governments involved feel that the appearance of action, or the process it entails, is of some broader utility. This trait is evident in other parts of the world,[2] but is particularly clear in Asia. Thus, a wide-ranging definition is needed to capture the political character of much of the region's cooperative activity – activity which might otherwise be excluded for its lack of substantive policy commitments.

Many previous studies have assumed that security-policy coordination involves three basic mechanisms. States either create collective security systems, collective defence systems or systems of cooperative security (sometimes described as the creation of a security community).[3] But this categorisation is of limited use here, because it focuses on multilateral forms of cooperation, while much of Asia's cooperation is bilateral. Also, such a schema only acknowledges reasonably firm diplomatic and strategic commitments, something that Asian states have often been reluctant to embrace. It also neglects the collaboration of a more competitive nature that has been evident recently, such as the implicitly anti-American geopolitical posturing of the SCO.[4] Asian states are involved in various cooperative endeavours, from dialogue on matters of common concern, through bilateral counter-terrorist intelligence sharing to multilateral military exercises. Meanwhile, many belong to military alliances predicated on conventional deterrence, which generate suspicion from non-participants.

Security cooperation in Asia is a distinctive combination of power-political and institutional approaches. Orthodox academic categories tend to favour one or the other, and find it challenging to integrate these two seemingly contradictory approaches. By defining security cooperation more broadly, as any form of joint action to advance a common security goal, one acknowledges the region's bilateral tendencies and its inclination towards a diplomatic and institutional light touch.

Security cooperation should not only be equated with multilateralism, even if this is the more ambitious and sometimes more significant mode. Bilateral forms need to be considered because they are important features of Asia's security setting, and because the way they interact with multilateral mechanisms is going to be one of the central challenges for Asian security policymakers in coming years. It is often assumed that bilateral mechanisms tend to be exclusionary – that they are targeted at, and prompt a competitive reaction from, non-members. Multilateral approaches, on the other hand, are considered more attuned to the interests of non-members and thus more benign in their effects. Asia's emerging strategic geometries do not fit this image.[5] Some bilateral mechanisms are quite cooperative, while other multilateral bodies have clear competitive dimensions.

There is no multilateral security institution in Asia – no NATO equivalent – with any significant means to ensure policy coordination or an operational dimension of consequence. Nonetheless, there are four distinct forms through which multilateral cooperation occurs:

- institutions, summits and other processes designed to build trust, foster regional confidence and improve information transfer, with a specific focus on security policy (such as the ASEAN Regional Forum or ARF);
- ad hoc functional initiatives designed to deal with, and limited to, specific issues or crises (such as the Six-Party Talks);

- broader institutional processes intended to cover an array of functional areas that have begun to include security (including APEC); and
- a growing number of informal and Track II security processes where academics, civil-society groups and government officials meet in a private capacity to discuss security collaboration. This has happened with the Council for Security and Cooperation in the Asia-Pacific (CSCAP) and Network of East-Asian Think Tanks (NEAT).

Meanwhile, there are four main forms of bilateral security cooperation in Asia today. The most influential is the series of bilateral alliance and quasi-alliance agreements that the US has with key regional states.[6] Secondly, bilateral agreements and commitments on functionally specific areas of cooperation, such as intelligence sharing, policing and counter-terrorism, have been increasingly important since the terrorist attacks of 2001. While these primarily focus on information sharing, they also involve more direct interaction, including personnel exchange and joint operations, such as the arrangements Australia has with Indonesia.

The third form is equally low-key. Since 2004, many states have been establishing formal bilateral security dialogues at often very high political levels. These include countries with a long tradition of shared interests and common action, and even those with difficult relationships, such as China and the US, or China and Japan. Finally, since the Boxing Day tsunami of 2004, countries such as Australia and Japan have been establishing bilateral mechanisms to improve operational coordination and interaction in humanitarian work, particularly disaster relief and the prevention of infectious diseases.

Thus, Asian states have at least eight multilateral and bilateral ways for cooperating on security. Some of these have been perceived as competitive, such as the Trilateral Strategic Dialogue. Others, such as the Shangri-La Dialogue, work to overcome, or at least mitigate, these competitive tendencies. (The subsequent chapter discusses these forms in some detail.)

There is genuine regional interest in increased security cooperation and an inclination to take some steps that may not have been possible in the past.[7] Several factors are generating this demand. At the broadest level, the transnational linkages created by the increased movement of goods, ideas, people and capital in the post-Cold War era of globalisation have not only brought economic opportunities; they have also made Asian states vulnerable in new ways.[8] Terrorists and organised crime groups may exploit legitimate networks of trade, finance and information technology. Travel, communication and agricultural production networks give infectious diseases new and rapid means to spread. The opportunities and vulnerabilities presented by globalisation are prompting states to recognise that new cooperative endeavours are needed to protect their interests.

Countries are exposed to new threats from abroad. Moreover, they have begun to perceive security challenges emanating from a wider array of circumstances. In the past, things such as soil erosion, water-catchment management or climate change would not have been considered security matters. Today, recognised security challenges can be transnational and multidimensional in character.

Finally, shifting power configurations in Asia, associated most obviously with the rise of China and India, the possible resuscitation of Russia's strategic weight and the relative strategic and economic difficulties of the US mean that there is considerable uncertainty in regional strategic thinking.[9] These three factors – globalisation, the changing character of security, and the uncertainties of power transition – are creating an unprecedented mood for cooperation in Asia.[10]

The appeal of 'architecture'

There are many different views as to what kinds of mechanisms are needed to get states to cooperate. Among the most popular instruments are international institutions. Yet it is not always clear what such security institutions actually are, how they are created or what they might involve. An intuitive understanding of international security institutions would see them as involving regular meetings among participants, the commitment of members to certain rules and procedures, expectations that members will conduct their security policy along certain lines and, if sufficiently resourced, a headquarters with a dedicated professional and administrative staff.

By contrast, the scholarly literature on international institutions has produced a somewhat leaner concept, one that sees an institution as something that ensures adherence by states to certain rules over time.[11] This sparse concept is intended to draw attention away from the superficiality of summits and buildings, towards the substance of policy interaction. From this perspective, institutions can exist without meetings, buildings or formal documentation; the institution exists so long as the participating states adhere to the rules.

From either the intuitive or the academic viewpoint, Asia's security institutions are not especially effective – with the notable exception of America's bilateral alliance and quasi-alliance relationships. They do not generate predictable forms of behaviour or common policy commitments that make states feel more secure. Furthermore, the array of different mechanisms created since the early 1990s to cope with the region's changing dynamics do not seem to fit neatly into either the intuitive or academic depictions.

Since 1994, the idea of 'security architecture' has become increasingly popular in the policy and public debate.[12] The popularity of the notion of an 'architecture', as distinct from multilateralism or institutions, is partly a reflection of the shortcomings of multilateral efforts to date. Asian states clearly exhibit a desire to cooperate to some degree; the mushrooming of cooperative efforts since the mid 1990s is testament to this. The turn to an architectural language reflects an attempt to find a more productive way forward. The idea of an 'architecture' also has the appealing combination of a neat rhetorical ring and an unclear policy consequence. In contrast to the settled meaning of cooperative security or security community,[13] the term has certain ecumenical qualities. Its normative blankness allows one to project almost anything onto it.[14]

But it is not only the combination of political expediency and weighty rhetoric that explains the idea's grip on those interested in cooperative security matters in the region. It is also because of the idea's complex connotations, which have been drawn from outside the security realm. A design-and-construction metaphor for broader responses to transnational problems came to prominence after the financial crises that rocked Asian economies in 1997, and spread to Brazil and Russia in 1998. Following these traumatic events, economists began to call for greater supervision of financial markets and more effective regulatory mechanisms. Many insisted that the conditions warranted a new international financial architecture.[15] There was much appeal in the orderly way in which the discipline draws together complex systems into a coherent and pleasing whole, especially given that the policy response to contemporary financial crises demands multifaceted cooperation from states, institutions, firms and markets.

At around the same time, security policymakers were beginning to take seriously the argument that significant threats to international security were emerging from a wide array of non-traditional sources.[16] Events during the past ten years, most obviously the terrorist attacks of 2001, have forced countries to recognise that security is a complex, multidimensional proposition. They realise that, to protect their interests, their policies need to respond to this new environment. Indeed for countries like Australia and New Zealand inter-state conflict appears to be very unlikely, and they see the main threats to their interests as emanating from these non-traditional sources.[17] Within Asia's complex strategic landscape, states perceive that their security policies need a blend of traditional and non-traditional approaches, including cooperation, information sharing and some policy coordination. So, unsurprisingly, policymakers and scholars have been attracted to the idea of 'an architecture' to capture the array of distinct, but interlocking, policy mechanisms that these new circumstances seem to require.

As a loose term for a collection of measures that seeks to secure the region, the idea of a security architecture is obviously appealing. But when one moves beyond the sketching out of regional possibilities into the more complex domain of real policy choices, there is a need for greater analytical precision. To that end, it is useful to consider how another region has responded to the changes in world politics.

Looking to Europe

The complex array of institutions, rules and alliance agreements underwriting European security are regarded as the primary example of a security architecture in the contemporary international system. It is also a relevant model for Asia because it has shown a remarkable capacity to provide non-traditional security functions in a complex setting. It has helped defuse significant and long-standing geopolitical tensions. In its peace-keeping roles in the Balkans and operations in Afghanistan, it has shown it can coordinate and manage international responses to humanitarian crises. It is an important buttress to the consolidation of democracy in Central and Eastern Europe. Notwithstanding recent tensions between NATO and Russia, the system's greatest achievement has been its ability to foster a strong sense of trust and common cause among countries that spent much of the post-1945 period on opposite sides of the Iron Curtain. Given that mistrust, strategic uncertainty, socio-political stability and transnational security problems, such as humanitarian crises and infectious diseases, are fundamental for Asian states, the conceptual and operational archetype of Europe's multidimensional system is obvious.

At the centre of Europe's security architecture lies NATO, which has transformed its strategic purpose since the end of the Soviet threat, and expanded its membership to include many former Warsaw Pact states.[18] Today, it not only maintains its traditional collective-defence function, but has added peacekeeping, peace-enforcement and stabilisation missions, both within and beyond Europe. It also serves to coordinate the security and defence policy of its members.[19]

Beyond the core provided by the new NATO, a range of collaborative measures gives the European architecture multiple centres of power, even if these centres are not necessarily of equal weight.[20] The core functions of NATO are supplemented by measures within the European Union (EU), the Organisation for Security and Cooperation in Europe (OSCE) and the Council of Europe (CoE). At the EU level, these include the Common Foreign and Security Policy (CFSP); broader moves around the European Security and Defence Policy (ESDP), such as the creation of the EU's Political and Security Committee, and of the EU's Military Committee and Military Staff; and the creation of the High Representative post.[21] The OSCE's activities include the promotion of dialogue and information sharing, the monitoring of borders and elections, and the coordination of counter-terrorism activities. The CoE adds a further political and diplomatic layer to these mechanisms.

The most important feature of the European system is a widely accepted consensus as to the sources of insecurity, as well as a basic commitment to the policies that best mitigate these risks. This involves a broadly inclusive attitude to security challenges, whereby policies are not organised around the targeting of specific states as threats, but instead seek to integrate security risks within the system.[22] The great majority of European states belong to an alliance founded on the view that members are not threats to one another; they share risks and do not perceive inter-state military conflict in Europe as likely in either the short or long term. For example, the 2003 European Security Strategy identifies transnational problems such as terrorism, the proliferation of WMD, organised crime and state failure as the pre-eminent challenges facing the region.[23]

The only caveat to all this relates to Russia. Since NATO's 1997 expansion, Russia has increasingly expressed its dissatisfaction with the European architecture, and the 2008 conflict in Georgia was partly driven by Russia's sense that the system was intended to constrain its influence. Yet even in this most troubled relationship, Europe has provided Russia with a stake in the system, in the form of the NATO–Russia Council.[24]

Europe has a multilayered and, at times, overlapping set of institutions and mechanisms, which provides a reasonably effective system for securing its political communities. While its origins lie in a military alliance intended to defend Western European states from Soviet attack, Europe's contemporary security architecture has been expanded and transformed, both in terms of the countries secured by its mechanisms and in its conception of security. It is this sort of complexity that is most often associated with the idea of a security architecture.

Grand and not-so-grand designs

While the association of the idea of an 'architecture' with the complex and multilayered system in Europe is widespread, there is no clear and settled meaning attached to the term. For the purposes of this book, however, it is important to clarify to what security architecture does and does not refer.

There are several different ways in which the term can be used. Perhaps the most common is to refer to a grand overarching security system created by a set of distinct cooperative mechanisms working collectively to achieve a common security goal. There are two subtly different forms that such overarching mechanisms might take. In the first, architecture refers to the deliberate construction of functionally distinct mechanisms with a clear-cut division of labour among them. The mechanism is created by states that share a set of security interests and have established cooperative measures to advance those interests.

A second possible variation brings institutions, dialogue forums and other processes of varying formality into a reasonably coherent association seeking to secure a specified geopolitical space from challenges to members' interests and values. Underpinning the association would be not only a shared set of interests among the member states, but also shared values and a consensus regarding the core threats to those interests and values.

The common values at the heart of such a system need not be liberal. Indeed, a future Asian security architecture of a grand kind may well not have liberal values at its heart. But whatever form it might take, this overarching architecture is a system of distinct, but interlocking, cooperative security mechanisms.

However, the grand vision, with its different possibilities, is only one way in which the term can be used. In some of the literature, 'security architecture' is used simply to refer to particular security organisations or mechanisms. As Australian National University scholars Robert Ayson and Brendan Taylor point out, some in Asia use the term to refer to the US bilateral alliance system, while others use it to refer to bodies like the ARF or the Six-Party Talks.[25] In this usage, architecture can be loosely deployed to refer to nearly any cooperative mechanism, from a bilateral agreement to a pan-regional dialogue forum. Even if one were to include only multilateral and cooperative endeavours, any region would be home to multiple architectures, and, of course, Asia would have plenty. The main problem with this meaning, apart from the distinct lack of precision, is that it does not really differ from existing terms, such as international institution, organisation, regime or alliance. In many respects, this usage is little more than a synonym and perhaps one of limited utility.

A third way in which the term can be used is simply to describe an existing, complex array of security policies. Security architecture can be usefully deployed to tidy up, for rhetorical or analytical purposes, a much messier reality. In Asia, the term is often used to describe the entirely unplanned and uncoordinated combination of unilateral security policies, bilateral alliances, agreements and multilateral processes, as if there were a considered logic at work.[26] Such moves serve a strategic or diplomatic purpose.

However, analytically, it is not especially useful to use the term as a catch-all label to essentially convey the world as it is. At the very least, the term implies some kind of broader purpose, or that some consideration or planning has gone into the interaction of the mechanisms. Using 'architecture' to describe an existing regional security order may even distract us from particular security challenges, by rhetorically tidying them away.

'Architecture' as a sign of purpose

Therefore, this book uses a fourth definition, which tries to draw together different elements associated with the idea of a security architecture. Asia does not have, nor are its policymakers especially interested in, a pan-regional, institutionally strong architecture of the grand kind, in either variation. However, there are efforts to go beyond the existing arrangements and to be more purposive about the regional order. The term is thus used to describe a broader security environment, in which distinct security mechanisms and processes interact with some degree of intent to ensure the stability of the regional order.

The use of the architecture label draws attention to the deliberate effort to establish mechanisms to secure the region with a range of different, and in Asia's case potentially contradictory, components. For example, an annual heads-of-state summit could be combined with lower-level dialogue forums that could coexist with, and indeed offset, the potentially negative consequences of existing military-alliance commitments. If these elements were deliberately brought together to provide a stable regional order, then one would have an architecture.

It could be that such an architecture would require the drawing together of different pre-existing strands with new entities, just as new buildings can be constructed out of a combination of old structures, pre-fabricated parts and entirely new elements. Importantly, the purpose of the security architecture is to stabilise an international order within a specified geopolitical space. While this can accommodate a certain amount of strategic haziness as to where the space begins and ends, the underlying geopolitical purpose of the system should be reasonably clear. The idea also has a degree of flexibility, and there are many different ways in which international agreements, processes and institutions can be designed and linked to achieve the architectural end.

In essence, architecture refers to a purposive effort to bring distinct security mechanisms together with a view to influencing the workings of the region's order. This approach makes clear that the institutionally heavy and top-down European model is not the only possible form of regional security architecture.

The question that this book seeks to answer is whether efforts to secure Asian states and societies through cooperative measures, and more directly through attempts to institutionalise a security architecture, are realistic in their ambition. Asia's security landscape today provides a complex, and sometimes contradictory, set of indicators as to the efficacy of security cooperation, and to the plausibility of an Asian architecture of the fourth kind outlined above. On the one hand, there has been a rapid expansion in the number and range of cooperative endeavours over the past 15 years. On the other, the underlying mistrust and mutual suspicion among the great powers, and the uncertainty of the lesser powers, continue to be dominant themes in Asia's strategic diplomacy. So can security cooperation reassure Asian states and societies? In short, what are the prospects of forging a viable and effective regional security architecture in the coming years?

CHAPTER TWO

The Current Regional Order

For most of the time since 1945, Asian states have tended to follow traditional approaches to their security policies. There were some low-key ambitions to forge multilateral security bodies in the early years of the Cold War, but most states have sought to secure their interests either through bilateral alliances or on their own. Initially, there was little appetite for explicit multilateral security cooperation. While groupings such as ASEAN did have an implicit security function, it was not until the 1990s that this became a much more conscious strategy.[1] Since the mid 1990s, this approach has been supplemented by a newfound enthusiasm for cooperation, both bilateral and multilateral, with a proliferation of institutional efforts unparalleled anywhere else in the world. Interestingly, this change in attitudes has not supplanted the established approaches; rather it is seen by many policymakers as an adjunct to their national defence policies and alliances.

A move towards multilateralism

A think tank in Tokyo, the Japan Center for International Exchange, estimates that in 2007 there were 277 multilateral intergovernmental meetings in East Asia related to security. These ranged from an ASEAN Regional Forum (ARF) Peacekeeping Experts' Meeting to the second ASEAN Defence Ministers' Meeting (ADMM) and sixth-round meetings of the ongoing Six-Party Talks.[2] As well as a significant increase in the range and scope of institutions, there has been an expansion in the number of states involved and even growth in the number of states leading these efforts, particularly since 2001.[3] Whereas the US used to be the prime mover for any regional security cooperation, China, Japan, ASEAN and Australia have each taken the diplomatic initiative since the turn of the century.

Enthusiasm for multilateral cooperation in almost all Asian states has produced an institutional proliferation that displays three distinct trends. Firstly, it has led to the creation of new institutions with security cooperation as their main purpose, such as the Shanghai Cooperation Organisation (SCO) in 2001. Secondly, it involves creating new groupings intended to foster wide-ranging policy cooperation, where security sits alongside other policy sectors, such as trade, investment and culture. The establishment of the East Asia Summit (EAS) in 2005 is typical of this trend. Thirdly, existing institutions and mechanisms have begun to include security on their agendas. Organisations such as the Asia Pacific Economic Cooperation (APEC) forum, which used not to address questions of security, are finding some value in bringing these matters to the institutional table.

Asian security cooperation ranges from the extensive and unfeasibly ambitious to the pragmatic and low-key. Despite this diversity, it is evident that this cooperation takes three distinct forms: open-ended intergovernmental groupings; ad hoc functional mechanisms; and non-traditional, sub-state modes of security cooperation.

Recent multilateral security bodies

ASEAN Regional Forum

The first clear sign that Asian states' thinking on security coop-eration had evolved came in 1994, with the creation of the ARF. ASEAN was established in 1967 to foster an international climate conducive to the attempts to forge strong states in poor and post-colonial Southeast Asian societies.[4] In the early 1990s, this geopolitical and economic grouping recognised the need for a more explicit focus on security matters. The crea-tion of the ARF reflected a recognition by ASEAN's members that cooperative security approaches needed some institu-tional foundation; it also demonstrated a realisation that the Cold War approach to regional security, both within ASEAN and beyond, needed to change. Today, the ARF comprises 27 countries (the ten ASEAN countries, the ten ASEAN dialogue partners, one ASEAN observer and six others; see Table 1, p. 73). It is intended to be the pre-eminent regional forum for security dialogue.[5]

At the outset the grouping had two basic functions. The first derived from ASEAN states' perception that the main threats to their security interests came from beyond Southeast Asia. This prompted the group to try to increase its capacity to influ-ence the security policy practices of non-ASEAN states in Asia, and particularly to influence the policies of the major powers. This served a dual purpose: the ARF was intended both to help lock America's interests into Asia – at a time when American disengagement seemed a very real possibility – and to draw an emerging China into multilateral processes. ASEAN states have long realised that Asian countries' geopolitical security is in many respects a function of the quality of the relations among the region's major powers. Ensuring that changing circumstances did not result in dramatic departures from the established patterns of great-power strategic relations was, and remains, a priority for ASEAN states. Equally, they recognised that their ambitions for the ARF required both Chinese and American participation.

The other basic aim was to start devising cooperative processes built on a wider conception of security than had been the regional norm. This included developing regional means of dealing with transnational security problems, such as piracy and environmental threats, which ASEAN governments were beginning to perceive as explicit security problems.

The ARF operates according to the core ASEAN norms of consensus decision-making. It has moved at a speed with which every member is comfortable, and has reflected the strong attachment of many of its members to the political and strategic importance of sovereignty and non-interference. It comprises a wide array of inter-governmental meetings at various levels. These range from the ministerial meetings at the annual forum and the annual senior officials' meetings, through regular seminars and conferences on specific issues such as cyber terrorism, peacekeeping or maritime security, down to regular meetings of the heads of defence-education establishments.

The ARF's extensive political and military inter-governmental meetings and working groups provide lines of communication for regular dialogue and opportunity to promote cooperation among security policy elites. The ARF framework also allows members to raise specific issues of concern and, potentially, to manage crises. However, this does not mean that the ARF has developed executive functions. Indeed, there is division within the ARF as to whether it should attempt to do anything more than improve political communication among its members. Such disagreement was evident among ARF members in 2008 during efforts to provide humanitarian assistance in Myanmar after Cyclone Nargis. The ARF's inability to contribute to the humanitarian relief effort, and a dispute among ARF members about how to respond to the crisis, demonstrated the grouping's difficulties.

From the outset, the ARF has had difficulty reconciling its ambitious agenda with political constraints stemming from the divergent interests and priorities of its wide-ranging membership and from the political limitations imposed by the 'ASEAN way'. In its 1995 concept paper, the ARF adopted a three-stage model for its evolution, moving from confidence building to preventive diplomacy and, eventually, towards a conflict-resolution capability.[6]

The first stage involved encouraging non-ASEAN states to accede to the grouping's 1976 Treaty of Amity and Cooperation (TAC) in Southeast Asia, as the treaty's commitment not to resort to the use of force seemed a sound basis for pan-regional confidence building and a concrete way to export ASEAN norms. However, members were cognisant of the difficulties of moving to the second stage of preventive diplomacy, particularly where unresolved territorial disputes were involved. Precisely what preventive diplomacy would involve was left deliberately vague. This was partly because a more active diplomacy would necessarily involve greater institutional capacity and autonomy, and this was politically unpalatable for many states, particularly core ASEAN states such as Malaysia and Indonesia, as well as some ARF members such as China. The third stage, conflict resolution, was deemed in 1995 to be a distant goal.

Some observers, such as Japanese policy analyst Akiko Fukushima, argue that the ARF has helped improve levels of regional trust.[7] Others, such as US Naval War College academic John Garofano, say it has helped to shape China's security-policy thinking into its present reasonably benign form.[8] In practice, however, the ARF has been unable or unwilling to move beyond stage one of its concept.[9]

The body has obvious structural shortcomings. For example, one of the region's major security challenges, the issue of Taiwan, cannot be addressed because Taiwan is not a member and China insists that it is an internal matter. The group's development has also been hamstrung by its broader institutional setting. ASEAN's mode of operation has considerably frustrated some members, particularly the US, Canada and Australia. Concerned about the glacially slow progress, and the over-valuing of process over policy, these powers have become somewhat disengaged from the process. Political principals from the US, for example, frequently fail to attend annual ARF meetings.[10]

However, several more recent developments perhaps provide faint glimmers of hope about the ARF's long-term prospects. At the July 2008 ARF meeting in Singapore, Chinese foreign ministry officials took many participants by surprise when they prompted discussion about ways in which the ARF could move toward adopting the preventive diplomacy phase of development. Following discussion at the ministerial summit, the issue only received oblique reference in the Singapore Declaration, which underplays its significance and demonstrates the unease among many members about the ARF taking on this role.[11] Some ARF members, most particularly the US, Australia, Canada and Japan, would prefer for the ARF to develop more concrete cooperative activities. While the confidence building and information sharing can continue, and in Asia's strategic landscape they are clearly needed, there is a sense among these more activist members that the current period requires something more.

China's willingness to tap this sentiment may help advance the ARF, but it also indicates Beijing's ambitions to regional influence. Perhaps it is also an effort by China to take advantage of a general American neglect of the ARF in the latter phase of the Bush administration. Another effort to move the ARF forwards came with the adoption of the Vision Statement of 2009[12] at Phuket, Thailand, in July, when the grouping tentatively set out a desire to make the ARF more 'action oriented' and to develop preventive diplomacy in priority areas. (It did not, however, commit the ARF to taking this next step in its institutional evolution.)

Another successful development was the conclusion of the ARF's first operational activity, the Voluntary Demonstration of Response on Disaster Relief (ARF/VDR).[13] This was a group of field exercises, held on 4–8 May 2009 in the Philippines, which brought together representatives from 25 ARF members, including the US.[14] Although relatively small, the exercise was significant because it represented a clear break with the ARF's 'talk-only' tradition.

Of course, the ARF has not suddenly been rejuvenated, and policy coordination even on humanitarian relief remains strongly couched in the language of non-interference prized by most ASEAN members. As Jürgen Haacke from the London School of Economics and Political Science also points out, the ARF may not be able to even maintain such activities, let alone expand its repertoire, because of a lack of interest among many members, particularly core ASEAN states.[15] Equally, humanitarian relief in response to the September 2009 disasters in Southeast Asia – Typhoon Ketsana in the Philippines and earthquakes in Indonesia – were handled as normal by states and NGOs. The ARF had no role to play in either, despite having conducted the ADF/VDR four months earlier on precisely such issues.

That said, recent ARF moves indicate a mood for change. This is partly prompted by the realisation that security cooperation limited to talk and confidence building will at some point cease to be of interest to many countries. It is also, to some

degree, sparked by the emergence of competition for cooperative forums created by the region's institutional proliferation.
The ARF remains the region's biggest multilateral security
organisation, but it is no longer alone and is not guaranteed
the continued diplomatic priority to which it has become
accustomed. Its future prospects look somewhat brighter than
they did several years ago. However, there are differing views
among members as to what the ARF should do, particularly
between the activists (such as the US, Australia, Canada and
Japan) and the rest of the membership. These differences will
limit the chances of any significant advance in concrete cooperative measures from the ARF.

Shanghai Cooperation Organisation
For the first seven years of its existence, the ARF was the only
multilateral grouping in Asia with an explicit focus on security cooperation. The 2001 creation of the SCO changed that.
Its establishment demonstrated growing interest from Asian
states for more institutionalised and multilateral forms of
cooperation. It also revealed a distinctly Chinese perspective
as to how this might be advanced. As the successor organisation to the Shanghai Five – adding Uzbekistan to the original
1996 grouping of China, Kazakhstan, Kyrgyzstan, the Russian
Federation and Tajikistan – the SCO is led by China and was
initially intended to help provide geopolitical stability to areas
surrounding China's West Asian border.[16] By the late 1990s,
instability across China's troubled Xinjiang province and the
former Central Asian Soviet republics appeared to be endemic,
so the demilitarisation and stabilisation of this strategically
significant region was the SCO's initial priority.[17]

Publicly, the SCO regularly declares itself opposed to the
three 'evils' of terrorism, separatism and extremism. However,
the organisation has moved beyond this. It now sees its other

main functions as counter-terrorism, the prevention of drug trafficking, and military cooperation and coordination. The SCO's immediate concern is to coordinate members' response to transnational threats, most particularly Islamist separatism. Some conservative Western analysts also suspect the organisation of representing a broader geopolitical gambit by China and Russia to jointly negate American influence in western Asia and to leverage this into a stronger global position. According to a classic Cold War dictum, NATO's goal was to 'keep the Americans in, the Germans down and the Russians out'. In a twist on this, the SCO's core business is sometimes said by such analysts to be to 'keep Russia in, the Americans out and Central Asia quiet'.

The SCO's Regional Counter-Terrorist Structure (RCTS) was established in 2003 (originally under the name of the Regional Anti-Terrorism Structure) and its executive council held its first meeting that October in the Uzbek capital, Tashkent. The following year, the RCTS created a permanent headquarters there. The RCTS is regarded by some analysts as having helped to reduce the incidence of transnational terrorism in Central Asia by improving policy coordination and sharing intelligence.[18]

The SCO has run joint military exercises since 2003 and joint counter-terrorism exercises since 2007. The latter included *Peace Mission 2007*, when all six members participated in exercises in the Russian Urals ahead of that year's SCO summit. The exercise showcased the growing, if still qualified, strategic linkage between Russia and China, as well as the People's Liberation Army's capacity to operate internationally and over some distance. It showed the SCO's growing ability to manage military cooperation and coordination, which is a notable achievement for an international security organisation. It also sent a clear political message to internal separatist movements.[19]

Since then, the organisation has begun to address issues such as the financing of terrorism and money laundering.

Beyond counter-terrorism operations, SCO activities have so far been ad hoc. However, there are efforts to devise a more formal mechanism to deal with illegal migration, control labour flows, and combat the trafficking and distribution of drugs,[20] with a particular emphasis on sharing information and intelligence related to these issues. Summits in 2008 and 2009 reiterated the desire to expand cooperation in this area. However, the group's efforts to constrain illicit flows of people and narcotics lack structure and have yet to amount to any significant policy coordination.

Although its founding document in 2001 hints at the use of the organisation for broader geopolitical purposes,[21] that geopolitical dimension has become increasingly important in the past four or five years. The SCO supported Uzbekistan's 2005 decision to terminate its lease to the US of the airbase at Karshi-Khanabad, and the group's growing ties with Iran appear to be intended as much to goad the US as to advance its regional security objectives. In its repeated support for different political and cultural systems, and its rejection of the 'export of political models', one sees none-too-subtle criticisms of American policy.

At the eighth SCO summit meeting, held in Dushanbe in August 2008, the organisation expressed support for Russia's incursion into South Ossetia and concern about America's missile-defence programmes.[22] There is a growing confidence among the members that the organisation is able to advance their international ambitions. This was most clearly articulated at the 2009 Yekaterinburg heads-of-state summit, where the six countries presented common positions on the larger questions facing the international system – such as the global finan-cial crisis, climate change and UN reform – and emphasised their shared commitment to basic principles of international conduct that reject key Western values, such as human rights and democratisation.[23]

Western strategists are also concerned that the SCO could become a gas cartel akin to OPEC. It has long been a Russian priority to ensure former Soviet republics do not undermine its own gas reserves' strategic potential, and it is possible that SCO members could coordinate their respective hydrocarbon industries. However, this is still a long way off, thanks primarily to Russia and China's divergent energy interests.[24]

Although, superficially, the SCO appears to present a new challenge to American and European interests, the reality is perhaps less alarming. Most SCO declarations are little more than posturing, and there is a long and difficult road to travel before the SCO becomes a kind of Central Asian Warsaw Pact. Indeed, it is not clear that the members have this sort of ambition. Importantly, underlying tensions between Russia and China will inhibit more extensive moves, particularly given that China has a much greater interest in good relations with the US than Russia does. Nevertheless, the shared interests among the membership over border control, internal stability, counter-terrorism and geopolitical positioning, their command of significant hydrocarbon reserves and Russia's growing confidence mean that the SCO has considerable potential to become more than an effective body for its members' common security concerns; it could also project their global strategic influence.

New dialogue forums
IISS Shangri-La Dialogue
Formally the IISS Asia Security Summit, the Shangri-La Dialogue is an annual meeting of defence ministers, military officers, bureaucrats, advisers and academic experts, which is organised by the London-based International Institute for

Strategic Studies (the producer of this Adelphi book). While it involves some non-government figures, it is primarily an exercise in first-track diplomacy where governmental representatives appear in their official capacities. (See Table 1 for a list of countries that have sent representatives.) Named after the hotel in Singapore where it has been held annually since 2002, the dialogue provides both formal and informal opportunities for policymakers and scholars to discuss diverse security concerns. Participants have used the formal speeches in a traditional fashion, namely to communicate policy or to signal defence and foreign-policy practices.

The Shangri-La Dialogue also allows for confidence building and information sharing in the more informal elements; it's a good opportunity for corridor diplomacy, that perennially under-appreciated aspect of multilateralism. It provides the chance for the region's defence officials to conduct an efficient round of meetings with control over what receives public attention. At the 2009 summit, there was a highly publicised meeting of the South Korean, Japanese and American defence ministers, held after North Korea's nuclear test that May. At the same meeting, the Australian defence minister conducted 27 separate bilateral meetings that were largely off the record. Few regional, or indeed global, gatherings provide such rich potential for defence and intelligence interaction.

The Shangri-La Dialogue has thus rapidly become one of Asia's most important annual summits. Many analysts regard it as having greater utility than the ARF, because of the consistency with which it is able to attract ministerial representation from all key powers. In its formal and informal elements, the Shangri-La Dialogue represents a telling development in regional confidence building. Among the reasons for its growing influence are its flexibility, the chance it offers for low-profile interaction and its targeting of ministers rather than national leaders. The tendency toward 'leader-led' groupings that is common across other East Asian multilateral bodies has politicised summits and made policy collaboration harder to achieve.

Moreover, the dialogue's relatively circumscribed agenda – security and defence policy detached from broader institution- or norm-building agendas – means that it does not suffer from mission creep or overly extensive aims. There is also no need for deliverables, such as statements or declarations, which more institutional mechanisms entail. Naturally, participants can choose to generate such agreements within their respective bilateral meetings, but there is no obligation to do so. Importantly, the dialogue does not have unrealistic ambitions. Because it is run by the IISS and is not affiliated with any particular power or set of interests, it is not subject to the concerns about underlying regional leadership ambitions that have hindered other groups.

Trilateral Strategic Dialogue
Another significant multilateral process reflects different trends. The Trilateral Strategic Dialogue (TSD) between Australia, Japan and the United States was initiated in 2002 at senior official level. In 2006, it was upgraded to an annual ministerial meeting, with follow-up meetings between key bureaucrats. The forum's formal purpose is to provide the two alliance partners with the opportunity to coordinate their security policy and to foster improved interactions between the three.

The creation of the TSD was partly a function of the ways in which the US alliance system in Asia-Pacific has undergone a subtle but substantive transformation.[25] Since 2001, Japan and Australia have tightened their strategic relations with the US; they have increasingly seen their bilateral alliances as having an international, not just a regional, function. The dialogue is intended to help these two US allies play a larger role within the alliance framework and to help facilitate intra-alliance, or 'cross-spoke', interactions across the traditional 'hub-and-spoke' structure of the alliance system.[26] It is no coincidence that Japan and Australia signed a formal security coopera-tion agreement in March 2007, the year after the first TSD ministerial-level meeting.[27]

Some analysts, including academic and former senior Australian defence official Hugh White, have interpreted this forum as a mechanism to coordinate American allies' policy on China.[28] In their view, it was created to help contain China's growing influence in the region. In 2006–07, there were efforts to bring India into the grouping and create a quadrilateral dialogue, and these seemed to confirm the containment suspi-cions.

However, changes in the domestic political circumstances of the three have led to the quadrilateral ambitions becoming downgraded. Both the Hatoyama and Rudd governments are particularly keen not to upset China, and the Obama adminis-tration has sought a more nuanced approach to the rising power. The meetings in 2007, 2008 and 2009 have been studiously low-profile and stuck to the relatively uncontroversial realms of disaster relief, humanitarian support and counter-terrorism.[29] But the Trilateral Strategic Dialogue does involve an underly-ing and potentially competitive approach to regional order, and might be used for a more assertive containment approach in the future. Members recognise this and have attempted to mitigate some of its more unsettling consequences, most obvi-ously the sense that China has of being contained.[30]

The Tripartite Summit
In December 2008, building on lower-level trilateral coopera-tion processes established in 1999, the three major Northeast

Asian powers of Japan, China and South Korea held their first 'Tripartite Summit' in Dazaifu, Japan.[31] At the second meeting, in Beijing in October 2009, the three agreed to work together to advance a sense of East Asian community, to embark on broader regional-institution building, and to establish a series of strategic dialogues, confidence-building measures, and military cooperation and exchange.[32]

This trilateral process is notable for bringing together three key regional powers whose mutual tensions have contributed to the sense of uncertainty throughout East Asia. The parties recognise both their mutual economic interdependence and the need for them to address their political conflicts. It is also significant as the first major summit in East Asia that does not include the Southeast Asian states of ASEAN.[33] If the putative Northeast Asian Security regime (see Chapter Four) came into being, and the Tripartite Summit delivered confidence to its members, ASEAN's days as the driving force for East Asian security could be numbered.

The dynamism of Northeast Asia's cooperative efforts, and its countries' economic and strategic weight, means that future Asian security cooperation may not be as constrained as it has been. This does not mean a sudden acceleration towards regional integration, but it appears that the dynamics of Asian security cooperation are not necessarily always going to remain subject to the effective veto of the ASEAN states.

How ASEAN will respond to this challenge remains to be seen. The Southeast Asian group has often been criticised for failing to make concrete achievements in the political and security sphere, but it has shown considerable aptitude for creative diplomacy. It is unlikely to willingly step back from regional processes.

Broader bodies now focusing on security

ASEAN Political–Security Community and ASEAN Defence Ministers' Meeting

Since its inception in 1967 ASEAN has had an important, if always tacit, security function. Many of its important early achievements were directed squarely at the security sphere, including the 1971 Zone of Peace, Freedom and Neutrality Declaration (ZOPFAN)[34], made in Kuala Lumpur, and the 1976 Treaty of Amity and Cooperation (TAC)[35] in Southeast Asia, signed in Bali. While regular ASEAN meetings avoided questions of international security, ASEAN began to take a security position in the 1980s, with its opposition to Vietnamese occupation of Cambodia.

In the early 1990s, the grouping recognised the need for a more explicit focus on security matters, but by creating the ARF (see section earlier in this chapter) it placed security concerns outside formal ASEAN structures. Yet throughout the 1990s, security matters leached into ASEAN processes. The grouping played a role in the early 1990s Cambodian peace process, was a key force behind the 1995 Southeast Asia Nuclear Weapon-Free Zone Treaty and, after a decade of negotiations, signed the 2002 Code of Conduct in the South China Sea with China.

At the turn of the century, particularly after the Asian financial crisis, there was also a realisation that ASEAN needed rejuvenation. To that end, the membership committed itself at its 12th summit in Cebu in 2007 to the creation of an ASEAN Community by 2015.[36] As spelled out in ASEAN Concord II,[37] this will comprise three pillars:

- an ASEAN security community (known since 2009 as the ASEAN Political–Security Community, or APSC);
- a social and cultural community; and
- an economic community.

The APSC envisages the advancement of political and security cooperation through work on political development, norm promotion, conflict prevention, conflict resolution and post-conflict peace building. The 2009 APSC Blueprint sets out in often quite specific terms how this will be achieved including, among many propositions, plans to advance democracy, protect human rights, improve transparency in defence policies, strengthen humanitarian assistance and improve concrete forms of cooperation to deal with non-traditional security challenges.[38] This is an ambitious programme which, if developed, will mark a significant break with past ASEAN practices.[39]

An important recent development under APSC auspices has been the inauguration of the ASEAN Defence Ministers' Meeting (ADMM). Since 2006, this regular meeting has brought together defence ministers to improve transparency, enhance confidence building, and achieve tangible defence and security cooperation.[40] The ADMM is a formal sector of ASEAN cooperation; it reports directly to the ASEAN heads of state and government, and it is intended to make concrete cooperative commitments among ASEAN member states. It is also intended to be the focal point for security cooperation outside the ASEAN membership.[41] To this end, it is complemented by a nascent 'ADMM-Plus' process, in which ASEAN defence ministers will regularly meet their counterparts from the organisation's dialogue partners, as well as other key parties (see Chapter Four).

The ADMMs have generated enthusiasm both within and beyond ASEAN. There is a sense that the ADMM can help achieve more concrete cooperation, particularly given the emphasis on dialogue and process in ASEAN's other security mechanisms, most obviously the ARF. It is also thought that a more limited forum, both in terms of functional scope and participating parties, is likely to yield more benefits. Thus far, the ADMM's chances of becoming a more action-oriented forum look good, as shown in the 2009 commitment to improve collective abilities to deal with non-traditional security challenges.[42] However, nothing concrete has yet been delivered.

The APSC appears to have three underlying purposes. Firstly, it is part of the process of reconfiguring ASEAN in response to the political, economic and strategic circumstances it now faces. ASEAN's broader reconfiguration represents an attempt to re-energise the organisation, which is facing competition in the market for multilateralism in Asia, from the Shangri-La Dialogue, as well as the Six-Party Talks and even the EAS (see sections later in this chapter). There are also internal divisions about core ASEAN principles and policy, particularly about the sanctity of the non-interference principle, which together provide incentive for organisational revitalisation. Secondly, the APSC is an attempt to consolidate and institutionalise the various ad hoc peace and security efforts with which ASEAN has become involved in the past decade; these include maritime security and counter-terrorism.

Thirdly, ASEAN states are keen to turn the rhetoric of a security community, which some of them have espoused for some time, into reality. It is increasingly clear that there are inter-state as well as transnational security problems within ASEAN, and that the grouping needs to respond to these problems. A consistent failure to act not only puts the well-being of member states at risk but also undermines the association's institutional credibility. Territorial disputes between Thailand and Cambodia over the Preah Vihear temple in 2008–9, and tensions that have been simmering since 2004 between Malaysia and Thailand over the separatist movement in three southern provinces.

The APSC has its critics. Some have already expressed scepticism about the extent to which it really breaks with ASEAN practice. Many doubt ASEAN's willingness to allow the kind of institutional autonomy necessary to achieve functional cooperation, let alone conflict resolution and post-conflict peacebuilding. The ambitions of the APSC in many respects fly in the face of ASEAN's traditional purpose: to provide inter-national reinforcement for the domestic programmes of strong state elites. Efforts to construct a rules-based system, in which comprehensive concepts of security are intertwined with prin-ciples of human rights and democratic governance, will give ASEAN an entirely new face and will disconcert many ASEAN member states' elites. Some scholars, such as the University of Swansea's Alan Collins, even argue that the APSC is unlikely to amount to much without a significant change in approach by traditional ASEAN elites, or without new opportunities for other groups, such as civil-society organisations, to influence ASEAN policy.[43]

The efforts to create an APSC hold out the potential for ASEAN's transformation. More immediately, however, they change the institutional setting of security policy within ASEAN, whereby ostensibly substantive political and security collaboration are envisaged as a central part of the association's activities. The APSC represents a shift in attitudes toward more substantive security cooperation and is indicative of the pres-sures for change within the group. It may be that we should be sceptical of ASEAN's capacity to change its ways. But even if the APSC is little more than business as usual, one must at least recognise that the nature of business has changed. Today, the forces that threaten the traditional aims of ASEAN states are no longer communism, but transnational security threats. How the organisation responds to these threats will have important implications for the association itself, its purpose, function and core principles. As such, the APSC marks an important phase in ASEAN's development.

Asia Pacific Economic Cooperation forum

Among all the existing institutions in the region, it is perhaps APEC's inclusion of a security dimension that tells most about changing attitudes to security cooperation. APEC's first ministerial meeting was held in 1989 and it quickly became a pan-Pacific body, meeting at national-leader level since 1993. As its name suggests, it was originally intended to focus on economic cooperation, with a particular emphasis on promoting trade and investment liberalisation. For its first decade it kept all non-economic matters off the table. In 1994, a *modus vivendi* was established with the ARF, whereby regional cooperation on security matters were referred to that ASEAN associate and APEC provided the focal point for economic matters.[44] The group expanded rapidly to include all key Asian and Pacific powers, plus several economies whose membership ultimately brought more challenges than benefits, such as Papua New Guinea and the Latin American economies. (See Table 1 for a list of all 21 APEC members). APEC also became heavily based on the leaders' summits, with these annual gatherings structuring the agenda in ways that hampered institutional effectiveness, particularly given the negligible administrative and bureaucratic support assigned to the grouping.[45]

By 2000, APEC had lost the enthusiasm of key members, especially the US, Australia, China and Canada. This was due particularly to its inability to make any headway in trade liberalisation, its core business.[46] At around the same time, it became clear that the economic linkages of globalisation brought with them considerable security risks, and that the institutions facilitating these economic connections were well positioned to respond to these new problems. As such, security matters have begun to assume significance at APEC, providing an ailing organisation with some much-needed momentum.

The annual leaders' summits have provided an ideal diplomatic opportunity to raise matters of security concern in ways that might otherwise have not been politically possible. For example, the 1999 Auckland summit hosted key meetings that paved the way for the UN intervention in Timor Leste (East Timor). At the October 2001 Shanghai summit, APEC condemned the 11 September terrorist attacks. It also facilitated the first face-to-face meeting between the Chinese and American presidents since the EP-3 spy-plane incident that April, which had badly damaged Sino-American relations. More generally, the 1997–98 financial crisis, the US terrorist attacks of 2001, and the 2002–03 outbreak of severe acute respiratory syndrome (SARS) in Asia put paid to the rigid division that APEC members had built between economic matters and security concerns.[47]

APEC now contributes to regional security cooperation in three ways. Firstly, under the technical-cooperation Senior Officials' Meeting, it has established the Counter Terrorism Task Force (CTTF). Under the CTTF is the Secure Trade in the APEC Region (STAR) initiative, established in 2002 to deal with the terrorist threat to trade. Intended to ensure the security of trade routes, ports and customs procedures, it is primarily focused on maritime trade, but also subsumes collaboration on airport security. STAR is an attempt to develop a permanent mechanism to help secure supply chains from terrorists, piracy and transnational crime.[48] Secondly, APEC attempts to manage non-traditional security concerns through discussion and practical programmes, most particularly over concerns about energy security and access to basic resources and commodities.[49] Thirdly, APEC summits provide excellent opportunities to deal with crises such as Timor Leste or the EP-3 spy-plane incident. Corridor security diplomacy has proven to be an unexpected benefit of the grouping.

ASEAN Plus Three

The primary concern of the ASEAN Plus Three (APT) grouping has always been economic cooperation. Despite this, from the start it was also intended to deal with any matter where the members thought there was potential for mutually beneficial cooperation. APT was established in 1996 and is best known for its currency-crisis arrangements, namely the Chiang Mai Initiative (CMI) currency-swap mechanism to help members respond to financial crises. Nowadays, however, negotiations over a possible APT free-trade area constitute its centrepiece.[50] The group comprises the ten ASEAN members (see Table 1) plus China, Japan and South Korea. This pan-East Asian membership, and the group's potential for wide-ranging forms of cooperation, means that it could serve as a vehicle for broader regional institution building.[51] In 2007 China made it clear that APT is its preferred venue for cooperative endeavours because of the group's constrained size and scope, although the fact that the US is not a member is also appealing.[52]

Unlike other broadly based groups, APT chose to make security dialogue an explicit part of its agenda from its first meeting. In 2004, the grouping decided to focus on transnational crime, establishing an annual ministerial meeting on the issue and regularly placing the topic on the agenda of the annual leaders' summit.[53] Under the banner of transnational crime, APT focused on eight issues: piracy, terrorism, arms smuggling, drug trafficking, money laundering, people trafficking, international economic crime and cyber-crime. Furthermore, the 2002–03 SARS outbreak prompted both a specific APT response to help advance coordination in combating the disease and preventing its return,[54] as well as ongoing work on infectious diseases.

During security discussions at the 2007 and 2009 leaders' meetings, APT leaders reiterated their commitment to work on infectious diseases and energy security. They continued their discussion and cooperative endeavours on transnational challenges, with particular reference to climate change, terrorism and other security challenges.[55] In 2009, support was reiterated for the Six-Party Talks on the North Korean nuclear crisis and the spotlight put on the H1N1 influenza (or 'swine flu'). This gives a sense of the discussion's breadth, although naturally discussion at leaders' summits does not necessarily produce policy change.

APT advances multilateral security cooperation in three ways. The most obvious is as a venue for discussing matters of common concern and for policy coordination through the regular channels it provides for dialogue among members. Secondly, it provides the opportunity for joint action and information sharing in relation to crises, as in the SARS outbreak in 2002–03. Finally, it serves a diplomatic function by building confidence among its members, as well as helping them to collectively shape developments in the broader region.

APT has considerable potential, but it has made more substantive policy contributions in the economic sphere, most obviously via the CMI. That said, the grouping is China's preferred vehicle for its regional cooperation, made clear not only in public declarations but also through Beijing's financial and infrastructural support of APT's Track II body, the Network of East-Asian Think Tanks (NEAT). So its potential implications for the regional landscape should not be downplayed.

East Asia Summit

The first EAS was held in December 2005, after the annual ASEAN summit in Kuala Lumpur. From the outset, the body was intended to cover economic, political and security matters. It was also meant to be geographically expansive and 'outward looking'.[56] In some respects, the EAS is a competitor to APT and, to a lesser degree, APEC. Its supporters hope to see it as the leading regional forum for broad-ranging multilateralism, and as a possible foundation stone for an 'Asian Community'. This view is most strongly held by Japan and supported to some degree by Indonesia, Singapore and Australia. However, is not held unanimously across the region. The competition between APT, APEC and the EAS in some ways reflects the competition for regional influence between each grouping's major supporter (China, the US and Japan respectively).[57]

Launched as a result of the APT's East Asia Study Group's report, which identified the need for a summit to advance cooperation in East Asia to promote stability and prosperity,[58] the first EAS summit of 2005 was prefigured by diplomatic wrangling over the group's membership and scope. Japan and most ASEAN states ultimately prevailed in their push for a broader, not exclusively East Asian, membership. They were able to do so because of concerns among all ASEAN states except Malaysia that China could come to dominate APT.[59] With this in mind, some see the EAS as a grouping intended to reduce China's regional influence, and to expand the geographic and functional scope of APT. It comprises all 13 APT members (see Table 1) plus Australia, India and New Zealand.

Thus far, however, the function of the EAS remains unclear and its future is uncertain. In a telling remark, a senior State Department official, when asked in 2008 about US attitudes to the EAS said bluntly: 'Tell me what it does, and I'll tell you what we think about it.'[60] But there are several features of the EAS that are of broader importance, beyond the geopolitical shadow boxing over membership and leadership. States that wish to participate in the EAS must first sign ASEAN's TAC. By forcing participants to commit themselves to a core ASEAN principle as a price of entry, the EAS has an important, if easily overlooked, security dimension. In requiring states to give guarantees to members, the EAS has a more robust foundation for security cooperation than any of the other broader groupings such as APEC, APT, the Shangri-La Dialogue and the ARF, even if its functional attributes are more basic.

The other security feature, and one that it shares with other bodies, is the opportunity for communication, information sharing and confidence building that comes from regular dialogue. The US is not a member, but it would give the grouping several advantages if it were to join, a prospect that has become somewhat more likely under the Obama presidency. Most obviously, it would bring all of Asia's major powers together in a single forum addressing both economic and strategic policy. It would also bring the US and China together in a multilateral framework with states that have acute interests in ensuring this relationship is smooth.[61]

In July 2009, the US signed the TAC and thus cleared the only major technical obstacle preventing its participation. To be clear, the US did not sign the TAC to join the EAS; rather it was part of signalling its policy intentions to Southeast Asian states. Nevertheless, this action has reduced the diplomatic costs of joining, a move that would enhance the security potential of the EAS. While thus far functionally stunted, the potential for the EAS to contribute to regional security cooperation is substantial, even if some way from realisation.

South Asian Association for Regional Cooperation
Another broader regional body that has added security to its work programmes is the South Asian Association for Regional Cooperation (SAARC). Formed in 1985, the SAARC was originally intended to promote intra-regional trade and investment to advance South Asian economic welfare, thereby helping to reduce the geopolitical tensions that have troubled the subconti-

nent since decolonisation. Its current members are Afghanistan, Bangladesh, Bhutan, India, the Maldives, Nepal, Pakistan and Sri Lanka. However, despite an ambitious programme and an extensive array of meetings on technical and political matters, the group has very little policy influence. This is mainly due to the longstanding mistrust between the two giants of the region, Pakistan and India. These two rivals have never been especially keen participants in what was originally a Bangladeshi initiative. But the SAARC's failure to progress is also caused by the poor administrative capacity of most members, as well as basic economic problems, such as incompatible trade structures.[62] Disputes and longstanding structural problems continue to limit progress. These also significantly constrain its ability to advance security cooperation.

There is, however, a realisation among the membership that things need to change,[63] and there have been some developments. In 1987, long before 9/11 and worldwide concern with the problem, the SAARC established its Regional Convention on the Suppression of Terrorism. To this it added, in light of more contemporary challenges, the 2004 Additional Protocol, which has led to some cooperation to limit the financing of terrorism.[64] In all subsequent summits, terrorism has been described as a core concern. Discussion in 2008 and 2009 sought to expand the ways in which other transnational security threats, such as energy security and organised crime, could be handled.[65]

The SAARC talks of 'crime' and 'criminality' when discussing these matters, to try to overcome the political difficulties relating to the term 'terrorism' in the stand-off between India and Pakistan over Kashmir. At a structural level, the SAARC has the potential to improve security cooperation in South Asia. However, the substance of cooperation, like the trade and financial sides of the SAARC, has been limited by its members' political differences and administrative shortcomings.

Functional security mechanisms

The Six-Party Talks

Alongside the continuing multilateral processes already discussed, functional security mechanisms have been created in Asia, either in response to specific crises or targeting particular issues. These have been among the more successful examples of Asian multilateralism and show that multilateral processes can work to resolve security problems in Asia under the right circumstances. The Six-Party Talks to resolve the longstanding dispute over North Korea's nuclear programme are among the most important developments in regional multilateral security cooperation. Involving China, Japan, North Korea, South Korea, Russia and the US, they were established to redress the failure of bilateral efforts to manage North Korea's nuclear ambitions.[66]

In 1994, the US and North Korea signed an Agreed Framework designed to freeze and replace the latter's nuclear programme. After this collapsed in 2002, the George W. Bush administration refused to deal with North Korea directly, in a decision as much driven by perceptions of North Korea's manipulative behaviour as it was by distaste for Clinton-era policies. This US stance, and Pyongyang's apparently cavalier attitude in ramping up tensions, created an extremely tense strategic environment with a strong sense that the diplomatic clash might spiral out of control. China took the lead in multilateralising the diplomacy in early 2003 and suggested that the bilateral structure of the 1994 deal be transformed into multilateral structure involving the six countries most immediately affected by the crisis. This led to the first of the Six-Party Talks in August 2003, ten months after the collapse of the Agreed Framework.

The talks are structured in negotiating rounds, held on a regular basis in Beijing. They are chaired by the Chinese representative, while the negotiators are high-level bureaucrats, usually deputy foreign ministers or equivalent. China's move towards a multilateral framework was driven by the need to get the US and North Korea to the negotiating table, even while America refused to meet in a bilateral forum. The participants also believed that a multilateral setting could provide a more effective means of structuring incentives, as well as monitoring and enforcing negotiated commitments.

The talks have progressed in an uneven fashion. They reached a nadir with the 9 October 2006 nuclear test. Yet a little over four months later, on 13 February 2007, the forum brokered a key deal in which North Korea agreed to cease its nuclear programme and return to the non-proliferation regime.[67] To a degree, North Korea has made good on its commitments, although not without some heel-dragging, for example, on disclosure of fissile-material stockpiles. However, all was very badly set back by the second nuclear-bomb test of 25 May 2009. Since then, North Korea has flirted with a return to the negotiation process and compliance with its previous commitments, but at the time of writing nothing concrete has been agreed. In short, therefore, the question of North Korea's nuclear capability is some way from being resolved to all parties' satisfaction.

The stuttering nature of the negotiations is a function not only of the general challenges of multilateralism, in which coordinating policy among multiple states is always fraught, but of the considerable differences among the six parties as to what they are trying to achieve and what they are willing to live with.[68] Even if they have actually not resolved the question of North Korea's nuclear capability, the talks are regarded as important for the relatively effective way in which they have defused the tensions on the peninsula. They are recognised as the only viable diplomatic path to a resolution of the issue to the satisfaction of the major powers. They also show unequivocally the importance and efficacy of Chinese diplomacy and China's pragmatic approach to multilateralism. Without Chinese leadership, the talks would not have been launched. Without the coordination of Chinese and American positions, the 2007 deal would not have been reached. The talks make clear that China is a status quo power, at least with regard to the Korean peninsula, and that it is an adroit diplomatic player whose strategic interests on the Korean peninsula are reasonably closely aligned to America's and Japan's.

Another reason the talks are particularly significant is because of a little-noticed clause of the February 2007 agreement, in which the parties agreed to form a working group to establish a permanent Northeast Asian security mechanism. Within the US State Department, and the Chinese and Japanese foreign-affairs ministries, there is a strong desire to use the basic framework and political capital built up by the talks to create an enduring security institution in Northeast Asia – a sub-region notable not only for its acute security problems but also for its almost complete lack of multilateralism.

Five Power Defence Arrangements
The region's oldest functional multilateral security mechanism, the Five Power Defence Arrangements (FPDA), is probably its least known. Established in 1971, the FPDA was designed to provide security guarantees to Malaysia and Singapore in the light of Britain's post-1968 military withdrawal from east of Suez. It was intended to reassure both new states, and was predicated on the principle that their security was mutual and indivisible. The five participants – Australia, Malaysia, New Zealand, Singapore and the United Kingdom – initially committed themselves to consult with one another in the event of external aggression against either of the two Southeast Asian parties. FPDA has involved annual ministerial meetings and other

regular dialogues, as well as military exercises among the five. There is a small permanent military headquarters in Malaysia.

In the twenty-first century, this essentially residual security arrangement has been rejuvenated and partially retooled, prompted by the changing strategic environment in Southeast Asia.[69] The emergence of transnational security challenges and the potential for non-state actors to exploit the jurisdictional complications of Southeast Asia's maritime environment prompted the FPDA – the only multilateral security grouping in the region with an operational dimension – to revitalise its agenda and broaden its focus.

In 2004, the FPDA defence ministers agreed to bring non-conventional threats into their exercises and scenario planning, with that year's joint *Bersama Lima* exercise focusing on anti-terrorist activities. Since then, the FPDA has included non-conventional security threats in its planning and exercises with a particular emphasis on maritime interdiction operations. It has sought to improve the defence linkages between the five countries, as well as broaden the range of government agencies involved countering terrorism and other transnational security threats. Overall, these changes have enhanced the grouping's strategic efficacy and political significance.

Malacca Strait Patrols
Indonesia, Malaysia and Singapore established the Malacca Strait Patrols in 2004 to try to overcome the jurisdictional difficulties complicating efforts to secure the heavily trafficked waterway. The group's creation was also prompted by the US Regional Maritime Security Initiative proposal, which envisaged US forces operating in the Malacca Straits. The Malacca Strait Patrols comprise coordinated trilateral sea patrols, a joint maritime–air patrol mechanism (which also includes Thailand) and formal intelligence sharing to support the two operational

dimensions. This last feature was established in 2006. While it is generally thought to have helped reduce piracy in the straits and to deter terrorism, the initiative has not fully overcome the problems of jurisdiction. For example, aerial surveillance crews must include participants from each country, and they must remain at least 48 kilometres off member states' coastlines.[70]

Proliferation Security Initiative

Although it is global in participation and focus, the US-led Proliferation Security Initiative (PSI) has been relatively well received by many Asian states. Nineteen Asian and Pacific states have been named by the State Department as participating.[71] Although not a formal signatory, Thailand has also taken part in PSI exercises[72] and publicly supports the principles. (See Table 1 for a list of all 20 regional participants.)

The PSI is a multinational attempt to limit the proliferation of weapons of mass destruction (WMD), primarily through maritime interdiction. The Bush administration established it in 2003 and initially it was supported by 11 American allies.[73] That September the group devised a set of principles on interdiction to try to assuage concerns about the PSI's legitimacy under international law.[74] Participation in the PSI involves three main types of interaction: discussion to determine priorities and the technical requirements of interdiction under PSI; training and exercises; and interdictions to seize WMD.[75]

In the Bush administration's second term, the US was actively courting wider participation in Asia, especially from China and South Korea, as well as Malaysia, Indonesia, Vietnam, India and Pakistan. These efforts proved futile because of PSI's controversial legal standing and the possible domestic political implications for partner countries. Some participants, such as Thailand, keep their actions very low-profile, and the PSI's future beyond the Bush administration is unclear. The Obama administration has indicated that it wants to institutionalise the PSI, but there has been no firm policy movement. There is enthusiasm for the PSI in some countries – particularly in Australia and, to a lesser degree, Japan – but this just under-lines the divergent threat perceptions and varying attitudes towards multilateral security efforts among Asian states.

Track II security multilateralism

An authoritative survey of Track II security processes describes them as 'unofficial activities, involving academics, think-tank researchers, journalists and former officials, as well as current officials participating in their private capacities'.[76] In part, the recent growth in Asian security multilateralism is a product of the support for informal dialogue and Track II diplomacy that has been evident in the region since at least the 1980 formation of the Pacific Economic Cooperation Council (PECC). Despite their general coolness towards international civil-society organisations, Asian states have been well disposed to Track II and other unofficial forms of interaction.

Track II processes attempt to devise new modes of coop-eration and to promote a broader sense of confidence. They have been important to the creation of new cooperative venues and their evolution.[77] For example, the ASEAN–Institutes for Strategic and International Studies (ASEAN–ISIS), a network of regional strategic-studies institutes, was instrumental in the creation of the ARF. Similarly, the Council for Security Cooperation in the Asia Pacific (CSCAP) has helped shape the ARF's institutional evolution. Track II meetings also occa-sionally include representatives from the private sector, such as members of the finance, manufacturing and professional services industries.

Track II activities are distinguished from other types of international gatherings, such as those of pressure groups or civil-society organisations, by their relationship to the policy process; they are intended to make some input, even if indirectly, into participating states' security policies. The intention is that by relatively informally bringing together representatives of these sectors, each with a particular interest in security policy, it is possible to generate new ideas about advancing common interests. One of the most important roles of Track II efforts has been as a venue to test the political viability of possible new schemes. Officials are able to speak more freely about plans and proposals when the political cost of frankness is much lower. Thus, governments may spend bureaucratic resources more effectively by determining in advance whether certain ideas are at all plausible. They can also benefit from the input of academics, journalists and think-tank researchers.

During the current decade, the number and range of Track II processes has increased significantly. The Japan Centre for International Exchange, which monitors these developments, notes that there were 284 such meetings in 2007.[78] The link between Track II and intergovernmental efforts can be seen in the three bodies apparently competing to be the premier regional institution. APEC, APT and the EAS each has a Track II body that is linked to its policy evolution. PECC continues to provide Track II support for APEC, along with APEC study centres located in each member economy. The China-based NEAT is linked directly to APT processes. The Japanese-supported Council on East Asian Community (CEAC) backs the EAS.

ASEAN has also shown some enthusiasm for linking intergovernmental security cooperation with Track II mechanisms, via its creation of ASEAN–ISIS in 1998. ASEAN–ISIS is best known for its annual Asia-Pacific round-table discussion in Kuala Lumpur.

Asia's Track II processes manifest both strengths and weaknesses. On the plus side, they offer the chance to test ideas and fly policy 'kites', and are valuable contributors to the habits of cooperation needed for more substantive policy coordination. They establish lines of communication that make contact between states more straightforward, and are particularly useful as alternative channels in times of crisis. Track II processes in Asia are generally thought to have been successful at promoting non-military approaches to security and broadening the security-policy debate in the region.[79]

But while low-key confidence building has been important, Track II methods have their drawbacks. Most obviously, they can be captured by governmental interests and their utility in the policy process can be easily undermined by government intrusion. CSCAP has particularly suffered in this way, where discussion of Taiwan and the involvement of Taiwanese participants have become increasingly fraught.

Bilateral approaches, old and new

Despite all their talk of multilateral and institutional approaches, Asian states actually predicate their regional strategies to a far greater degree on traditional military means, organised either bilaterally or nationally. Foreign- and defence-ministry officials spend much time and energy on multilateral consultative committees, working groups and summits. But the impact these numerous mechanisms have on participating states' security and strategic policies is often negligible. The most important elements of security cooperation in Asia are not multilateral institutions, but the bilateral alliances and quasi-alliance arrangements that the US has with many states in the region. America's forward projection of its military power, its bilateral alliances and its security partnerships provide the most significant force stabilising the region's current order.

Any analysis of Asia's nascent security architecture that only considers multilateral mechanisms will miss its most important feature. Alongside the American alliance system, a range of new bilateral mechanisms has emerged since 2000, adding further bureaucratic complexity to Asia's security landscape. This trend shows that Asian states often have highly flexible regional-security policies. It also demonstrates their lack of confidence in aspects of multilateralism.

America's Asian alliances

America has had a substantial military presence in Asia since 1945.[80] This has been organised around a series of bilateral alliance and alliance-like relationships with states in Northeast and Southeast Asia (see Diagram 1, p. 76). Today, this military presence, and its supporting security relationships, is thought of as reassuring by most scholars and analysts. It prevents regional rivalries from boiling over and keeps the arteries of Asia's growth – its sea lanes – open. The notion that the US is Asia's 'least distrusted' power – usually attributed to former Singaporean prime minister Lee Kuan Yew – retains its relevance.[81] Since its withdrawal from Vietnam and the normalisation of Sino-American relations in the 1970s, America's regional security role has been key to the long-term geopolitical stability, and thus economic growth, of East Asia.

Apart from a brief period in the early 1990s, when recession and the end of the Cold War prompted a strategic turn inwards, the US has maintained a consistent commitment to being the most powerful military force in East Asia and to organising its security links in the region almost entirely on a bilateral basis. In Asia, the US has avoided the multilateral means that it uses to manage its European security engagement through NATO. Meanwhile, it cannot adopt a unilateral posture in the region, primarily for reasons of geography. Given its extensive economic and political interests in Asia, the US requires stability. It believes it cannot rely on an indigenous Asian balance (or set of institutions, for that matter) to produce this. Washington also recognises that any significant disruption of Asia's regional order would require an American response, and it prefers to maintain regional stability routinely rather than to respond only in emergencies. Its Asian policy is also part of its global strategy, which has been arranged on an explicit policy of overwhelming global military preponderance since the first Bush administration.[82]

The US has opted for a bilateral structure for its security relationships[83] because they are a more efficient means of organising strategic policy than multilateral arrangements, and because of basic geographic considerations. Equally, given the inequality in size and capabilities among its Asian partners, the 'hub and spoke' pattern, as it has often been called, provides the centre with maximum opportunity to influence proceedings. It avoids the risk of junior partners collectively attempting to shape policy and reduces the risk of entrapment for the senior partner.

The role played by the US, and its bilateral structure, is generally accepted by most regional powers, both for the aggregate good of regional stability, as well as for particular, valued features of the current order. Of these, the two most notable are the openness of the maritime environment, so vital to regional prosperity, and the way in which it has kept Japan from playing a significant regional strategic role, about which China and others would be uneasy.

The US maintains regional stability by deterring states from using military power to advance their interests, or to challenge the strategic status quo, and by sufficiently dominating the maritime environment so that sea lanes of communication are reliably open and not vulnerable to control by any other power. The bilateral relationships, although often couched in the language of values and rights, are primarily products of shared interests and involve a basic strategic transaction. America gives its partners narrow security guarantees, promises broader regional stability, and provides access to US intelligence and restricted defence material. In return, it receives diplomatic and political support. It also gets material benefits, such as bases and facilities, and funding in support of the US presence that help it achieve its broader strategic objectives.

Although it maintains its Cold War core, the alliance system is subtly changing. Australia and Japan are tightening their relationships and binding themselves over the longer run to the US. Meanwhile, South Korea is beginning to loosen its relationship, for example disaggregating the joint command of the two countries' forces on the Korean peninsula. However, security links between the US and regional states continue to play a key role and remain the central load-bearing feature of the region's strategic balance. Although some questions are being raised about the utility of military power in America's security and strategic policy,[84] the US remains broadly consistent in its approach to the region. Most Asian states also prefer an American-brokered regional order to the alternatives.[85] Even China recognises that it benefits considerably from the US presence, and that it would pay a heavy price in any significant shift away from the current order. At the very least, China would need to do more to secure the sea lanes on which its prosperity depends.

A new burst of bilateralism

The US alliance system is the oldest and most important form of bilateralism in the region, but it is not the only one. Even while multilateralism has gained favour and pace, there has been a new set of bilateral moves in security policy. This has involved two distinct types of bilateralism. One form includes functional cooperation and treaties; the other involves dialogue intended to promote communication and confidence building. The former has tended to occur between countries with evident common interests and linkages. The latter involves countries whose fractious relations have been the staple diet of Asia's strategic analysis.

Prompted by many of the same sort of transnational developments that have spurred the growth in multilateralism – such as terrorism, crime, pollution and population flows – many states in Asia are forging a range of bilateral functional cooperative agreements. For example, in 2007 Japan and Australia signed a bilateral security declaration that aims to improve joint operations relating to transnational security challenges. The two countries now hold regular joint meetings of defence and foreign ministers.[86] Australia and Indonesia signed a new security treaty in 2006, and many countries in the region have established formal bilateral channels for cooperation on counter-terrorism and other transnational measures. Many Asian states have supplemented their multilateral approaches with bilateral measures as well.[87] These include a wide range of commitments, from the sort of technical information exchange one might expect among proximate neighbours, such as between Indonesia and Australia, to broader defence initiatives such as India and Japan's maritime cooperation. Although these bilateral relationships do not impede efforts to advance multilateral security cooperation, they are of more than marginal consequence. Asian states are responding to new security challenges with a mix of bilateral and multilateral approaches.

Perhaps more intriguing has been the growth in security and strategic policy dialogue between states that once had strained, if not acrimonious, relations. That US–China relations are presently on a very good footing, particularly considering the long-standing mistrust between the two, is in no small part due to the extensive range of dialogue and communication established during the second Bush administration, which has been built upon by the Obama administration. The highlight of this is the high-level strategic dialogue involving both countries' defence, foreign and finance ministers. These talks have focused on improving economic relations, cooperating to combat terrorism and managing nuclear proliferation.[88]

Meanwhile, Australia and China held the first of their annual strategic dialogue meetings in February 2008,[89] only a few weeks before the eighth round of Japan–China strategic dialogues in Beijing.[90] In addition, Japan and South Korea have initiated regular meetings on strategic policy at vice-ministerial level.[91] The US established a defence framework agreement with India in 2005, and the civilian nuclear deal passed by the US Congress in 2008 allows India to access US and the Nuclear Suppliers' Group civilian technology and fuel. Japan and India are also exploring ways of improving their bilateral defence and security ties. China has established bilateral military links with Cambodia, Bangladesh, Indonesia, Laos, Thailand and Vietnam. Vietnam has established dialogues with the US and Indonesia, and has proposals for similar arrangements with Japan and South Korea. Anecdotal evidence suggests that there are also many confidential security-related meetings among Asian states particularly relating to intelligence cooperation.

From this necessarily cursory overview, it is clear that while multilateral security cooperation is a growth business, it is not the only means through which Asian states are cooperating on matters of security policy. For many Asian states' the increasingly transnational nature of security challenges and the broader insecurities that derive from globalisation are together prompting a broader reconsideration of the utility of cooperation, particularly, but not exclusively, through multilateral means. There can be no question as to the need for more effective cooperation. Yet the continuation of bilateral approaches, particularly the US alliance system, together with strategic competition related to the significant degree of flux in the region's strategic balance, means that Asia's security setting is now shaped by a somewhat uneasy blend of competitive and cooperative processes. A combination of power-political and institutional approaches is shaping the contours of the regional order.

Table 1: **Participants in Asia's multilateral processes**

Grouping	Est.	Membership	Security Issues Covered
ASEAN Political-Security Community (APSC)	2004	ASEAN member states: Brunei, Cambodia, Indonesia, Laos, Malaysia, Myanmar, Philippines, Singapore, Thailand and Vietnam	One pillar of the ASEAN community; to promote political development, comprehensive security, norm diffusion, confidence building, defence transparency, humanitarian assistance and conflict resolution and post conflict
ASEAN Defence Ministers Meeting (ADMM)	2006	ASEAN member states: Brunei, Cambodia, Indonesia, Laos, Malaysia, Myanmar, Philippines, Singapore, Thailand and Vietnam	Central part of the APSC; to promote concrete cooperation to improve defence transparency, humanitarian assistance, combat non-traditional security challenges
ASEAN+3 (APT)	1996	ASEAN member states – Brunei, Cambodia, Indonesia, Laos, Malaysia, Myanmar, Philippines, Singapore, Thailand and Vietnam – plus China, Japan and South Korea	Dialogue on: transnational crime; infectious disease prevention; energy security
ASEAN Regional Forum (ARF)	1994	ASEAN member states – Brunei, Cambodia, Indonesia, Laos, Malaysia, Myanmar, Philippines, Singapore, Thailand and Vietnam; plus ASEAN dialogue partners – Australia, Canada, China, the European Union, India, Japan, New Zealand, South Korea, Russia and the United States; plus , Bangladesh, Mongolia, North Korea, Pakistan, Sri Lanka and Timor Leste	• Regional confidence building • Dialogue on common areas of concern. Issues covered in conferences seminars and summits: maritime security; energy security; cyber-terrorism; transnational terrorism and crime; peace operations; WMD proliferation • Disaster relief exercises, such as ARF/VDR • Moves towards preventive diplomacy
Asia Pacific Economic Cooperation (APEC)	1989	ASEAN members – Brunei, Cambodia, Indonesia, Laos, Malaysia, Myanmar, Philippines, Singapore, Thailand and Vietnam – plus Australia, Canada, Chile, the People's Republic of China, Hong Kong SAR, Japan, South Korea, Mexico, New Zealand, Papua New Guinea, Peru, Russia, Chinese Taipei and the United States [a]	• Leaders' meetings forum for security dialogue • CTTF: Secure Trade in APEC Region (STAR) initiative
East Asia Summit (EAS)	2005	APT members – Brunei, Cambodia, China, Indonesia, Japan, Laos, Malaysia, Myanmar, Philippines, Singapore, South Korea, Thailand, Vietnam – plus Australia, India and New Zealand	Dialogue on energy security; infectious diseases cooperation; and national disaster mitigation
Five Power Defence Arrangement (FPDA)	1971	Australia, Malaysia, New Zealand, Singapore and the United Kingdom	Defence of Malaysia and Singapore; cooperation on transnational security challenges and counter terrorism; military exercises
Malacca Strait Patrols	2004	Indonesia, Malaysia, Singapore [b]	Joint patrol of the Malacca Straits

Table 1: **Participants in Asia's multilateral processes**

Grouping	Est.	Membership	Security Issues Covered
Proliferation Security Initiative (PSI)	2003	Participating Asia-Pacific states: Afghanistan, Australia, Brunei, Cambodia, Canada, Fiji, Japan, Kazakhstan, South Korea, Kyrgyzstan, Mongolia, New Zealand, Papua New Guinea, Philippines, Russia, Singapore, Sri Lanka, Tajikistan and Uzbekistan [c]	Prevention of WMD proliferation
Shanghai Cooperation Organisation (SCO)	2001	China, Russia, Kazakhstan, Tajikistan, Kyrgyzstan and Uzbekistan [d]	• Border stabilisation in Central Asia • Military exercises on counter-terrorism • Policy coordination to combat: drug trafficking; transnational crime and transnational terrorism
Shangri-La Dialogue	2002	Representatives have come from: Australia, Bangladesh, Brunei, Cambodia, Canada, China, France, Germany, India, Indonesia, Japan, Laos, Malaysia, Mongolia, Myanmar, New Zealand, Pakistan, Philippines, Russia, South Korea, Singapore, Sri Lanka, Thailand, Timor Leste, the United Kingdom, the United States and Vietnam	• Confidence building and communication • Corridor diplomacy. Issues discussed: energy security; disaster relief; infectious diseases; regional security institutions; terrorism; WMD proliferation; defence policy making processes
Six-Party Talks on the Korean Peninsula	2003	China, Japan, North Korea, Russia, South Korea and the United States	• Denuclearisation of Korean Peninsula • Transformation into ongoing Northeast Asian security regime
South Asian Association for Regional Cooperation (SAARC)	1985	Afghanistan, Bangladesh, Bhutan, India, the Maldives, Nepal, Pakistan and Sri Lanka	• Regional convention on terrorism suppression • Confidence building among South Asian states
Trilateral Security Dialogue	2006 (2002) [e]	Australia, Japan and the United States	Coordinate strategic and security policy. Issues discussed: humanitarian assistance and disaster relief; counter-terrorism; WMD proliferation; shared strategic goals
Tripartite Summit	2008	China, Japan and South Korea	Series of strategic dialogues and confidence-building measures; personnel exchange; natural disaster relief

a. APEC has member economies.
b. Thailand also participates in the initiative's joint maritime–air patrols.
c. Although not a formal signatory, Thailand has participated in some PSI exercises.
d. Mongolia, Iran, India, and Pakistan have observer status, while Belarus and Sri Lanka are SCO dialogue partners.
e. First held at sub-ministerial level in 2002, then regularly held at ministerial level from 2006.

Table 2: **Overlapping participation in Asian multilateral processes**

Country	APEC	ARF	APT	ASC	EAS	FPDA	PSI	SAARC	SCO	SLD	SPT	TPS	TSD
Afghanistan													
Australia													
Bangladesh													
Bhutan													
Brunei													
Cambodia													
Canada													
Chile													
China													
EU													
France													
Germany													
India													
Indonesia													
Japan													
Kazakhstan													
N. Korea													
S. Korea													
Kyrgyzstan													
Laos													
Malaysia													
Maldives													
Mexico													
Mongolia													
Myanmar													
Nepal													
NZ													
Pakistan													
Philippines													
PNG													
Russia													
Singapore													
Sri Lanka													
Tajikistan													
Thailand													
Timor Leste													
UK													
USA													
Uzbekistan													
Vietnam													

SLD Shangri-La Dialogue
SPT Six-Party Talks
TPS Tripartite Summit

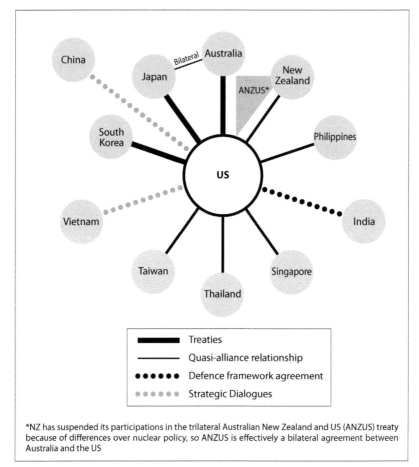

Diagram 1: **Main US military-security alliances**

CHAPTER THREE

Understanding the Complexities

Asia's strategic landscape is in a state of flux,[1] and the region's security mechanisms are responding by changing. Today's blend of multilateral and bilateral processes, and the combination of institutional and balance-of-power approaches, seems unlikely to remain as it is for any great period. If we are to understand the likely future trajectory of regional security, and if policymakers are to make informed choices about how security cooperation might foster regional stability, we need to understand the political and strategic implications of the current setting and the place of cooperative mechanisms within it.

Evaluations of security cooperation in Asia tend to the extreme. Some analysts argue that it achieves almost nothing. They say that the habits of cooperation and norms of restraint are unable to influence the preferences of Asia's powerful states, and that regional stability is a function of traditional factors shaping state choices, most particularly power and perceptions of threat.[2] Others contend that multilateralism is already forging Asian security communities with a concomitant stability driven by shared values, common interests and 'we-feeling'.[3]

As the preceding discussion has shown, things are not as straightforward as either position implies. Powerful states' interests are not constrained or shaped to any significant degree by many of the region's cooperative measures. Yet this does not necessarily mean that all cooperation is pointless or that existing mechanisms yield zero security returns. Some efforts, such as the Six-Party Talks, have played an important role in dealing with particular security challenges. Others, such as the ASEAN Regional Forum (ARF), have achieved less.

Although security cooperation in Asia is sometimes caricatured as lacking in substance, Asian states have collaborated on security matters to achieve important results. The UN-run INTERFET mission in Timor Leste (East Timor) in 1999 had a strong Asian dimension,[4] the SARS outbreak in 2002–03 prompted unprecedented levels of cooperation on quarantine, immigration and customs procedures,[5] and the 2004 tsunami showed that rivals were capable of putting aside some concerns to help provide aid to devastated parts of Southeast and South Asia. These responses involved unprecedented levels of cooperation. They also showed the clear shortcomings of the region's existing institutional framework.

Whatever the weaknesses of the cooperative mechanisms created thus far, most Asian states display a strong and seemingly genuine interest in cooperative measures of various kinds. Therefore, the two pressing issues are to determine which aspects of regional cooperation function well and which do not, and why it is that, in the face of this demand, the failings of supply are so manifest and seem likely to continue.

Identifying the ingredients of success

Evaluating the efficacy of security cooperation can be difficult. There are no neutral criteria against which one can measure a grouping's achievements, nor are there established international standards to which one can turn. Conclusions thus ultimately depend on what the analyst values in any given grouping. For example, if one puts a priority on process as a benefit in and of itself, one will reach very different conclusions about the efficacy of ASEAN than if one were to emphasise substantive policy coordination. In passing judgement, one needs to select reasonable benchmarks that take into account what the mechanism is trying to achieve. Groupings have quite different aims. Some are about dialogue and confidence building, such as the ARF; some seek more substantive interaction, such as the ASEAN Defence Ministers' Meeting (ADMM); others are problem-oriented, such as the Six-Party Talks. So benchmarks need to be sensitive to this diversity.

One means to gauge efficacy is to judge the extent to which members regard the grouping as usefully contributing to their respective regional security objectives. This can be ascertained partly by members' enthusiasm for the body and the extent to which scholars and analysts recognise this attribute. Another yardstick is the degree to which the grouping is achieving its own goals. These are not just the aims articulated in public – which can be at some remove from the internal goals, for political reasons – but also those recognised by analysts and policymakers. For example, the ASEAN Political-Security Community (APSC) has as a public goal the creation of a security community in Southeast Asia by 2015. Among ASEAN members, however, this is not considered realistic; the real aim is to make progress towards concrete cooperation on security matters in seven to ten years. It is impossible to precisely quantify institutional efficacy using these or any other indicators, but they do provide a useful means of gauging the effectiveness of the region's many multilateral security initiatives.

The intergovernmental multilateral security bodies that are most widely supported and that are doing most to achieve their own goals are the Six-Party Talks, the Shangri-La Dialogue, the ADMM within the APSC, and the Shanghai Cooperation Organisation (SCO). The least effective groupings are the South Asian Association for Regional Cooperation (SAARC), the East Asia Summit (EAS), the Proliferation Security Initiative (PSI) and ASEAN Plus Three (APT). Mechanisms performing in the middle of these extremes include the Five Power Defence Arrangements (FPDA) and the Trilateral Strategic Dialogue (TSD). The ARF arguably could be slotted into this middle category. Recent attempts to move it to the preventive-diplomacy stage of development,[6] and operational activities such as the ARF/VDR disaster-relief exercise in the Philippines in May 2009, may yet rescue if from a lack of enthusiasm, most evidently expressed by policymakers and analysts from non-ASEAN states. However, it is too early to determine whether these efforts will succeed, so it is prudent to put it in the 'least effective' category for the time being.

The more effective bodies share three features, which together provide an insight into why some groups have enthused their members and made in-roads into security-policy coordination, while others have not. Size is not one of these indicators of success. While smaller groups might be considered more likely to generate results, maintain momen-tum and enthuse members, in reality there is no clear-cut correlation. Some small groups have not fared especially well, while some larger bodies are making reasonable progress.

Instead, a body's effectiveness seems to be related to its organisational and functional attributes. At present, Asian states prefer security cooperation that:

- is functionally specific;
- is narrow in its focus; and
- largely operates without the publicity and pressure that the regular involvement of heads of state brings.

Recent developments in multilateralism show that function-ally specific cooperation, with clear and concrete goals, can work to make concrete contributions to the security aims of Asian states. The Six-Party Talks are a good example of this. Of course, the primary aim of the negotiations – the denuclearisa-tion of the Korean Peninsula – has not yet been achieved, and the talks' detractors point out that they have failed to prevent two nuclear tests. Yet the talks have succeeded, if only spas-modically, in de-escalating the nuclear crisis. Perhaps more importantly, they have established a widely supported diplo-matic modus operandi for crisis response in Northeast Asia. This is not only because of the commitment to the process shown by China and the United States, but also because the talks have focused on a specific issue. Without North Korea's nuclear ambitions, it is difficult to imagine the five external powers coming together regularly to build confidence, share information or otherwise cooperate on broader security matters. But faced with an issue of common and acute concern, the participants have forged a viable diplomatic mechanism that may yet develop into an ongoing process.

Of course, the region's many venues for security dialogue usually do not focus on a single concern like the Six-Party Talks do. Nevertheless, their relatively narrow and targeted agenda is of more interest to Asian states than that of wider-ranging dialogue forums. Both the Shangri-La Dialogue and the ADMM are more highly valued by policymakers and politicians than the broader ARF or the EAS. They both receive greater political priority from participants, and they are seen by policymakers and analysts as having a particular utility. Perhaps the clear-est illustration of this is the regular and extremely high-level participation by the US in the Shangri-La Dialogue compared with its involvement in the ARF. This preference appears to be because such dialogues are functionally focused on defence and strategic policy, and are not linked to larger pan-regional economic or community-building projects. The narrower security focus reduces the prospects for distraction and complication. It also means that information sharing, confidence building and the fostering of personal relationships are all much more likely to occur, because the relevant politicians and policymakers are present. These groups are also better positioned to maintain momentum and gain the diplomatic involvement needed to foster the kind of regional confidence that existing security mechanisms have not yet really achieved.

The third common element of the more successful multilateral groupings is political. The level at which a grouping meets and the place of national leaders within the institutional process are vexing questions in all forms of multilateralism. Asian multilateral groupings, both security and economic, have tended to be structured around annual summits where heads of state and government meet to advance the body's work. Involving national leaders provides important political capital and the capacity to make decisions swiftly. It brings the sort of clear government commitment that is never entirely certain in lower-level meetings. Yet there is a price. The media spotlight that follows leaders is rarely conducive to the kind of complex negotiations required in multilateral endeavours. Moreover, organisations may fall hostage to the domestic political interests of the particular leaders. And having a leaders' group structuring a multilateral institution's work programme almost invariably limits its autonomy, reducing its capacity to produce cooperative benefits.

Presently, national leaders dominate the meetings of the Asia Pacific Economic Cooperation (APEC) forum, the APT and the EAS. One must not neglect the role of Senior Officials' Meetings (SOMs) in these mechanisms, nor the role of 'sherpas' who allow the leaders to determine declarations in a relatively short time. Indeed, the dialogue and confidence-building ambitions of these groups are in many respects advanced more effectively by SOMs and 'sherpa' interactions than by summits of national leaders. Nevertheless, leader-led bodies are clearly more constrained than other groupings, both by the public attention they attract and by the fact that their highly visible domestic responsibilities leave national leaders less room for political manoeuvre.

The SCO has an annual summit involving national leaders. However, it also has some institutional autonomy in its Regional Counter-Terrorist Structure (RCTS), which manages member states' interaction in their joint fight against transnational terrorism, coordinates intelligence sharing, and is responsible for devising joint responses to common security challenges (although this last is still largely hypothetical). The ARF and Trilateral Security Dialogue involve foreign ministers; the ADMM convenes at defence-minister and senior-official level, as does the FPDA. The Six-Party Talks involve senior diplomats with no direct participation by ministers. The Shangri-La Dialogue welcomes ministers, military chiefs and permanent heads of defence ministries, along with non-official delegates such as academics and think-tank analysts.

None of the more effective groupings directly involves national leaders, but as the ARF has shown, their absence alone does not guarantee success. The involvement of top politicians can undermine effective progress in security cooperation; the ability to negotiate politically sensitive deals, and to develop confidence and useful habits of cooperation, is made more complex if national leaders participate directly. There is a place for leaders' summits in security matters. They can cement deals, raise the profile of certain issues and break deadlocks. However, making them the central focus, rather than just part of a broader process, seems to be counterproductive.

What doesn't work

Just as there are features shared by the more successful multi-lateral groups, certain factors appear to make things worse. Thus far, regional experience with ambitious visions for top-down, institutionally strong forms of security cooperation has not been encouraging. The grand hopes for regional community lurking behind APEC, the APT and the EAS have all been kicked down the road. Australian Prime Minister Kevin Rudd's calls for a summit-level Asia-Pacific Community[7] since June 2008 have met with a generally cool regional response.[8] Even Australia's closest ally, the US, is not especially supportive.[9] While regional powers recognise the need for more effective cooperation, there is little enthusiasm for expansive institutional structures attempting to manage economic, political, cultural and strategic affairs across the Asia-Pacific region.

A second difficulty is that many states appear to have lost some of their enthusiasm for dialogue as a process in and of itself. This is not to deny that information sharing, confidence building and transparency in security policy are useful features of the region's many groupings. However, because of the wide range of dialogue forums, their overlapping membership and policy spheres, and an ineffective division of labour among these groups, the region may be approaching the point at which dialogue for its own sake is now subject to diminishing returns. This seems to be particularly so with the larger bodies associated with community building.

Much of the thinking behind the 1989 formation of APEC was that trade and investment links would tie states' interests together and promote a sense of common cause, which would in time translate into more concrete policy linkages in more sensitive sectors. The notion that policy coordination in less controversial economic spheres might eventually produce security benefits at a low political price was understandably popular in Asia. Given the widespread mutual mistrust between the region's countries and acute sensitivities over sovereignty, an indirect and incremental approach to security cooperation seemed to be the only way forward.

Yet these ideas have not fared well. APEC was unable to make much headway with its economic programme because of the voluntary structure of its liberalisation programme and a lack of leadership.[10] So its indirect security-policy benefits were stillborn. Moreover, both the Japan–China and US–China relationships have shown that shared economic interests do not automatically produce a transformation in security policy. These bilateral relationships involve remarkable economic complementarity and very obvious mutual interests. Despite this, both are accompanied by difficult, and at times fraught, political relationships.

Equally, the growing sources of insecurity over the past ten years have also made indirect approaches to security cooperation somewhat redundant. While it may have been reasonable to try to improve strategic relations in Asia via trade promotion and investment facilitation in the early 1990s, today's policy climate requires more direct action. The sorts of mechanisms needed to deal with nuclear proliferation, environmental collapse and transnational terrorism – to take three examples of new threats – will not come from the slow binding of interests through the promotion of economic interdependence. This is not to say that broader efforts are useless, simply that the sorts of security threats prompting much of the contemporary interest in cooperation require rather different action.

Finally, states no longer feel the need to disguise cooperative measures, even if they are still hesitant in their commitments. Experience has shown that putting off the harder discussions until more conducive circumstances arise will result in little more than an enduring state of policy deferral.

Lack of trust and investment

Given the widespread regional interest in security cooperation, why have Asian institutions and multilateral efforts thus
far failed to meet this demand? Multilateralism may provide
useful ways of dealing with some challenges, but mistrust
between states, poor institutional structures, a lack of confidence in multilateral processes and other broader factors are
preventing multilateral efforts from reducing states' sense of
insecurity to any great degree. States are responding to the
changing security setting – the shifting distribution of power,
nascent strategic competition and transnational security challenges – by pursuing cooperative measures. However, they are
also hedging their bets with more traditional power-political
approaches. They do so because of a lack of confidence in the
ability of institutions to provide the kinds of guarantees that
the current strategic environment appears to require.

The single most important impediment to more effective
multilateral security cooperation is the lack of trust across the
region – particularly the distrust, if not outright rivalry, that
exists among the major powers. Effective multilateralism,
whether economic or security-related, requires leadership. A
state, a concert of powers or an institutional mechanism like
the European Commission is needed to provide the leadership
for substantive cooperation over any significant period. Not
only is leadership lacking in Asia; distrust of those powers in a
position to take the initiative means that others will react warily,
and may even contest their moves, if any of them promotes a
particular vision.

Thus, even well-intentioned efforts to promote a sense of
common cause run the risk of unintended consequences. This
was seen most clearly during the lead-up to the first EAS.
Efforts to build a regional sense of common cause were badly
undermined as Japan and China's dispute over membership

soured the initial summit. (Japan ultimately prevailed with its wish to have Australia, India and New Zealand included, in order to dilute China's influence over a narrower, exclusively East Asian group.)

One way around this may be to have lesser powers such as Singapore or Australia act as non-threatening leaders. Experience with this has not been heartening, especially considering the cool response to the Australian prime minister's proposal for an Asia-Pacific Community. Yet part of the reason the Shangri-La Dialogue has been relatively successful is that it is run by an effectively neutral body, the London-based IISS.

States also have widely divergent perceptions of the nature and sources of security threats across the region. Coupled with the objective diversity of these security challenges, these different interpretations of threat make it extremely difficult to move beyond basic levels of confidence building or narrow groupings (in terms of both function and membership).

Moreover, Asian countries and other powers involved in Asia have increasingly divergent opinions as to the value of dialogue and the usefulness of process as a security good in its own right. America, Australia and Canada have always been somewhat sceptical of its utility. Japan and China are not as doubtful, but have become less enthusiastic than the ASEAN states are. Even within ASEAN there appears to be subtly different attitudes between the more activist countries and other members towards the value of process as a security good.

Finally, the time and money devoted to multilateralism is miniscule in comparison to that spent on traditional security measures. Asian states have not matched their rhetorical endorsement of multilateralism with political and fiscal commitment. Indeed, as a comprehensive study has shown, there is a large gap opening up between what Asian countries say about their defence priorities and what they do. Their rhetoric is rich in the language of cooperation and non-traditional security policy. Meanwhile, they are increasing spending on offensive military capabilities.[11] Until that gap is narrowed, it is unreasonable to expect any significant change in the ability of Asia's multilateral security efforts to reduce Asian states' sense of insecurity.

Untamed growth: overlap and crowding

As Tables 1 and 2 show, the proliferation of security cooperation efforts in Asia has produced a remarkable array of groupings, whose work covers everything from counter-terrorism in Central Asia to information sharing on maritime piracy in Southeast Asia and efforts to secure trade routes around the Pacific Rim.

One feature of this tremendous expansion in security cooperation has been the almost complete lack of coordination. The region's sheer geographic extent, the diverse security interests of Asian states and underlying tensions among many key powers all militate against effective coordination. However, the lack of an efficient division of labour, or even basic efforts to coordinate the various cooperative endeavours, has important implications.

Indeed, it could be said that the region has an unusual problem: there are too many security-related institutions. This has led to substantial overlap in membership and agendas, producing considerable replication and, in some instances, the risk of redundancy. For example, with the exception of several powers from outside the region, those who participate in the Shangri-La Dialogue also all take part in the ARF – sending their defence ministers to the former, while their foreign ministers attend the latter. All members of the EAS attend the ARF, and they are, with the notable exception of India, also members of APEC.

Overlap is also evident in the many institutions' agendas. Counter-terrorism is discussed in almost every forum, while energy and resource security has become a common focus since the dramatic increase in oil prices in 2005 and food prices in 2006. While there is a clear need to place these matters high on agendas, there is apparently no coordination among the various efforts and a high degree of replication, especially in dialogue forums.

In part, the proliferation of security mechanisms, and the overlap this has produced, is a result of institutional politics. In some cases, groupings have used security matters to try to revitalise their members' interest or to create new institutional dynamism. This is most obvious in the case of APEC. It is also evident in the EAS and the SAARC, which have included security matters because of broader ambitions and as a way to make themselves more appealing to increasingly jaded members.

This suggests a more basic point. Whereas groups like APEC used to make themselves appealing to prospective members by not talking about security matters, the failure to consider security would today doom any broader collective endeavour in the region, where policymakers rightly recognise the consequences of trying to isolate economic and security questions. Security discussions are seen as necessary to any form of broader regional policy coordination, yet the problems already discussed appear to limit the capacity of cooperative endeavours to give Asian states an improved sense of security.

A further source of the replication among groupings is the absence of consensus across Asia as to what the region is, what its pressing security challenges are and what security function groupings should be serving.[12] It is hard to avoid the conclusion that more effective security cooperation requires a new institutional framework.

It is tempting to see these circumstances as an example of market oversupply, where countries' interests will eventually ensure that an appropriate division of labour emerges between groupings. However, this is perhaps an overly positive prediction, because institutional proliferation imposes significant costs. The scarce bureaucratic resources that states devote to the complex and time-consuming diplomacy of security cooperation may be spread too thinly to produce worthwhile results. With multiple summits for raising issues and forging consensus, the chances appear low of achieving any significant gains in substantive security. Cooperation in this sensitive policy sphere requires not only common interests but also long-term diplomatic commitment and sustained momentum.

Finally, while many Asian powers, particularly the ASEAN states, once placed a high value on security dialogue for its own sake, the growing competition between the increasing number of institutions is reducing this premium. It is also evident that regional powers, paradoxically, sometimes use cooperative measures as proxies for their broader rivalry, such as occurred at the EAS. Thus, the prospects for Asia's regional security to be enhanced by cooperative endeavours are not as great as they may first appear. Not far beneath the veneer of diplomatic common cause presented by the cooperative mechanisms national rivalries remain.

Twin-track policies

Alongside Asia's extensive multilateral security mechanisms is a series of bilateral security arrangements, of which the US alliance system is the most significant. As a mechanism to maintain stability by deterring Asian powers from using force to advance their ambitions, it is plainly not a cooperative mechanism giving all parties a stake in the regional security system. It maintains stability through America's capacity to prevent states from entering into competition and is rightly credited as being the foundation of Asia's recent three decades of geopolitical stability. The system rests on America's capacity, both fiscal and political, to maintain overwhelming military predominance, a situation that makes Asian states vulnerable to shifts in American policy. A realisation of this long-term vulnerability partly explains current efforts to devise new means of maintaining a durable regional order.

More broadly, the underlying tensions between cooperative mechanisms trying to build trust and a sense of common cause, such as the ARF or the EAS, and more exclusionary mechanisms, such as America's alliances, makes for a curious situation. The alliance system is predicated on the credible threat of force, and it produces a reliable regional order. Meanwhile, many of the multilateral mechanisms that attempt to embody trust and common cause are incapable of providing such stability or security. Some of the multilateral groupings are inclusive and do not aim to target specific states as threats. Others, such as the SCO, have an exclusionary logic, even if it does not target anyone in particular.

At present, security cooperation involves bilateral and multilateral approaches that are competitive, as well as bilateral and multilateral mechanisms that are cooperative in their underlying mode of operation. How these different modes relate to one another is, and will remain, a significant challenge for policymakers in the region. Does bilateralism inhibit multilateral mechanisms, or can states successfully pursue twin-track policies? Is it reasonable to rely on a competitive logic to maintain order while trying to transform the system into something quite different?

In international trade policy, there is a long-running debate about the relationship between multilateral and preferential trade agreements. Some argue that bilateral agreements, because of their exclusive character, hinder realisation of the wider benefits of multilateral agreements. Others argue that, because of their smaller size, bilateral agreements can act as the vanguard for the multilateral system.[13] This debate – between those who see bilateral agreements as impediments to multi-lateralism and those who feel that they can facilitate it – can be instructive when considering security arrangements in Asia.

In essence, the trade-policy debate relates to the broader implications of institutional design. The central point of differ-ence between multilateralism and bilateralism in trade policy relates to the beneficiaries of liberalisation. Under the rules of the multilateral system, all parties are accorded the same treatment; thus any liberalisation agreed under that system is available to all parties without discrimination. On the other hand, bilateral agreements only extend advantages to members. Bilateral agreements tend to be concluded much faster than the multilateral arrangement, but they divert bureaucratic resources away from, and reduce the political support for, the multilateral system.

In principle, the two seem inimical. Yet, in practice, the economic and political relationships between bilateral and multilateral trade policies are less starkly at odds than the theory suggests. Some preferential agreements do help advance the multilateral trading system, such as 1983's ANZCERTA agreement between Australia and New Zealand, in which liberalisation procedures for trade in services developed between the two countries became a model for application at the multilateral level.

In the same way that there is an uncertain relationship between open and more discriminatory trade agreements, the link between cooperative and competitive security mechanisms is not entirely clear-cut. They each have aspects that may be inimical to the success of the other. Equally, each has advantages that play out over different timescales: the competitive bilateral framework appears more suitable to immediate needs and preferences, while cooperative multilateral approaches seem better suited to longer-term problems, although they are strategically and diplomatically more complex.

The present blend of bilateral and multilateral security mechanisms, as well as the gap between the rhetoric of cooperation and increased defence expenditure on offensive weapons, indicates a continuing mistrust among key powers. There is neither consensus on the character of security threats faced by regional powers nor on the appropriate policy responses. While a proliferation of cooperative arrangements and an expansion of more competitive approaches may appear to be contradictory trends, the experience with trade-policy arrangements shows this is not necessarily the case. Bilateral arrangements do not always come at the costs of multilateral ones; the two can interact in a mutually reinforcing fashion. Having a range of security institutions and mechanisms built on different logics is not automatically a zero-sum game.

The different elements and divergent rationales do make the creation of a coherent and singular security architecture unlikely. But the way in which the various types of mechanism affect each other and the broader regional order depends on both institutional design and diplomatic management. Security mechanisms are political instruments. They are not mechanistic processes that automatically respond to circumstances; rather they can be adjusted to changing circumstances. Through prudent and creative diplomacy, ways can be devised whereby groupings that may appear to be contradictory in their logic can interact in mutually beneficial ways.

Hedging their bets

It is precisely this realisation that has led states to include multilateral and cooperative security approaches within their broader hedging strategies. Hedging is a part of many Asian states' defence and security policies, and is usually associated with their responses to the shifting power dynamics resulting from China's rise. American policy toward China over the past decade or so is illustrative of this approach. The US uses deterrence to shape China's policy choices while simultaneously pursuing diplomatic and economic engagement.[14]

'Hedging' more generally refers to ways in which states try to manage risk by adopting policies that provide some kind of insurance against a particular event occurring. It attempts to reconcile potentially contradictory strategic policies, to reduce the risk of either approach failing to achieve its aims. Examples of strategic hedging in the cooperative policy domain include Australia's tightening of its bilateral military relationship with the US at the same time as joining the EAS (and somewhat reluctantly signing the Treaty of Amity and Cooperation, or TAC), and China's decision to play a leadership role in the Six-Party Talks while simultaneously supporting the SCO, with that group's assertive geopolitical posturing.

Hedging is increasingly shaping the dynamics of security cooperation across the region. It appears safe to conclude that states are trying to maximise the opportunities for cooperation, particularly in areas relating to non-traditional security threats, while minimising the risks that cooperation poses to their broader security interests. For example, the dialogue and confidence-building measures of the ARF around common and comprehensive security have security benefits for members. But these are not sufficient to prevent some of those countries from acquiring ballistic missiles or procuring F-16 fighter jets.

States wish to cooperate, and in some areas such as infectious diseases and piracy, they have very little choice. They see the benefits that cooperative mechanisms produce, for example increased transparency, improved confidence or technical coordination for counter-terrorism purposes. But they are unwilling to rely on multilateral processes for fundamental concerns. This stance is driven by the uncertainty pervading the region's strategic balance, as well as by a lack of confidence in the region's existing multilateral security processes. Asian countries' insecurity is such that some of their policy choices, most particularly the acquisition of offensive weapons, sit uneasily with the confidence-building and other cooperative measures they are pursuing.

Hedging, as a conscious policy choice, naturally limits the possibilities of cooperation and reduces the security payoffs of existing cooperative efforts. It does so by diverting bureaucratic and fiscal resources across multiple approaches. It also undermines efforts to build trust. It is a policy response to uncertainty, but one that does little to ameliorate that uncertainty. At times it even exacerbates it.

Much of the multilateral cooperation in Asia today is driven by efforts to manage great-power relations. In particular, it is an attempt to ensure that China's growing power does not destabilise the region by producing rivalry with the US and, to a lesser extent, Japan. A desire to manage great-power relations was behind the formation of the ARF and the EAS and drives discussions about an Asia-Pacific Community. Yet the improved lines of communication, information sharing and efforts to build trust that are intrinsic to this approach are limited by the policy choices of many of those countries encouraging multilateralism. In strengthening their military alliances – which are implicitly intended to constrain China's military influence in Asia – Australia, Japan and, to a lesser degree, Singapore and Thailand, are hedging their bets. This limits the capacity of multilateralism to improve regional stability.

That hedging is a potential drag on multilateral security cooperation should be self-evident. It would be alarming if policymakers in Canberra, Tokyo, Singapore and Bangkok were oblivious to the ways in which the conflicting elements of their policies limited the efficacy of their efforts to build security multilaterally. However, there is clearly a belief in regional capitals that the broader consequences of hedging are not entirely negative. Hedging can be a prudent policy that allows states to deal with change and regional uncertainty in a manner that can reduce the destabilising consequences of more cautious policy choices. With careful coordination, a policy of hedging allows states to incrementally shift their policy positions and reduce the risks of misapprehension by other states, who might otherwise interpret such moves as having negative implications for themselves.

The current setting in the region can be seen as the result of states seeking to reduce the scope for misunderstanding from other states, by improving information exchange and communication, and by optimising the effect of policy speeches and other signalling mechanisms to demonstrate intent and strength of commitment. Meanwhile, they retain power-political strategies at the centre of their defence and security policies. Asian states lack real confidence in multilateral processes and thus seek to secure themselves through traditional military approaches. But they also recognise that this traditional approach has risks, and multilateral processes are a way of mitigating these.

Of course, hedging is by no means a panacea. Risk mitigation is, and will remain, a very difficult diplomatic business in Asia, with its diversity of states, long history of animosities and newly enhanced ambitions. Hedging is unlikely to provide a basis for regional stability if the multilateral processes fail to bring necessary levels of information (and the inefficiencies of the current system make this a real prospect) or if the power-political strategies create too much uncertainty and rivalry.

However, it is important to recognise that hedging may be able to reconcile Asian states' power-political strategies with their weak multilateral processes to generate regional stability, at least in the short term. The institutional and power-political paths to regional order are not, despite appearances, necessarily contradictory. They can interact productively, and the hedging evident in most states' security policy is partly a result of this more optimistic assessment.

The growth of cooperative efforts is encouraging, in that it recognises the need for regional states to adjust their policies to cope with evolving circumstances. However, the profusion of multilateral institutions may complicate the management of these circumstances. At present, the creative tension between the institutional and power-political approaches is helping to sustain the region's relatively stable order. However, the inefficiencies of the multilateral processes, as well as their profusion, may make this equilibrium increasingly difficult to maintain.

A fractured architecture

At the 2008 Shangri-La Dialogue, Singaporean Minister of Defence Teo Chee Hean described the state of Asia's security cooperation in relatively positive terms. He noted that the region's security architecture had three layers, comprising wide-ranging multilateral groups, narrower functional bodies and bilateral mechanisms.[15] It is certainly true that the region has these features, but this assessment seemed to imply a great deal more coherence and policy efficacy than is the case. To see it as an orderly, if still sub-optimal, set of mechanisms overlooks the palpable competitive tensions that exist across the region, among and even within some institutions. It equally underplays the policy stagnation of some multilateral groupings and understates the extent to which Asia's regional security institutions do not assuage Asian states' strategic uncertainty.

That said, in today's complex set of security mechanisms, one can discern an architecture of sorts. But the levels of mistrust and rivalry between states across the region mean this architecture might best be described as partial or 'fractured'. What does it mean to describe the region as having a fractured security architecture, and what are the implications of this for regional order? Given the convoluted array of groupings that presently exist, the juxtaposition of competitive and cooperative strategic dynamics, and the many major-power rivalries and territorial disputes, there is a temptation to conclude that the strategic balance is maintained through power-political means, with cooperative endeavours being little more than window dressing. However, such a pessimistic conclusion is unwarranted.

The panoply of security bodies existing today does confer security benefits, and without these bodies the region would be distinctly less secure. The Six-Party Talks have helped manage a complex and volatile situation in a reasonably effective fashion, notwithstanding setbacks. The ARF and the Shangri-La Dialogue have provided useful forums for managing the regional consequences of China's rise. Efforts to combat transnational terrorism have been unambiguously advanced through several multilateral bodies. In any future security crisis in Asia – perhaps the collapse of Workers' Party rule in North Korea, another outbreak of SARS or an escalation of the Thai–Cambodian border dispute – there would be no shortage of forums in which regional states could define multilateral responses.

Security cooperation plays an important part in the region's strategic balance; it figures in discernible ways in the security-policy thinking of Asian states. Yet, as the term 'fractured architecture' suggests, the region is not maximising the security benefits that multilateral cooperation promises. Asia has a set of institutions and mechanisms that helps stabilise regional relations and, on a limited scale, helps to promote human security. But these institutions have no clear division of labour. They overlap in a messy and uncoordinated fashion, which undermines their own policy efficacy. Asia's security architecture is also 'fractured' by the competition and rivalry undermining the efficacy of cooperative efforts. Most importantly, it is so described because there is no intent for the disparate mechanisms to interact to shape the region's order.

The fractured nature of the region's security architecture has important implications for the way we understand its security environment, as well as for the future of Asian security cooperation. Order has long been organised around the United States' regional security and economic roles. The US has maintained the region's strategic balance, as well as being the leading investor and primary market for exports. Since the late 1990s, this has begun to change, and the region is now beginning to develop a hybrid security order.[16] The bilateral alliance system retains its centrality, but a fractured security architecture overlays this.

Most Asian states recognise the long-term limitations of relying on the US alliance system as the main stabiliser of the region. Yet there are quite different perspectives on how the regional order might evolve. One view is that US power will remain key to regional order, and the future challenge will be to reorganise the structure of America's regional power projection for the post-Cold War strategic landscape. In this view, using military alliances as a stabilising force retains its centrality, but the policy framework needs to be refined for an Asia of multiple major powers.

A different approach might focus on the transnational and unorthodox character of the most acute challenges now facing the region, for which the set of bilateral security alliances predicated on military deterrence is of little use. From this perspective, the region needs new means to coordinate state action to deal with these transnational problems.

A third, more classical position might consider the region as best served by the creation of a genuine balance of power, where order would be produced by strategic competition between several major powers, as opposed to the current military predominance of the US. This balance, assuming it were stable, might provide a basic foundation for cooperation to deal with non-traditional and transnational security challenges. A fourth perspective might argue for the creation of a concert or directorate model, in which great powers collectively take responsibility for the management of order.

These diverse stances on the region's changing strategic circumstances are by no means contradictory. Aspects of each can be discerned in the current range of bilateral and multilateral cooperation efforts, and in the beginnings of a hybrid order. There have been some subtle shifts in the alliance system, with a strengthening of the Japanese and Australian alliances (expanding some of their functions beyond the region) and the initiation of some intra-alliance interaction. However, its basic organisation, function and purpose remain largely intact. China, India and, to a lesser degree, Russia are beginning to provide hints as to what a more evenly spread distribution of power in Asia might look like. The region is thus at a crossroads.

The verities of Asia's recent past offer little guidance for the medium to longer term. In some respects, the emerging hybrid order appears to involve the continuation of America's alliances as the cornerstone of the region's stability, but at the same time power is being redistributed in ways that challenge the assumptions underlying the alliance system. Layered across these developments are the multilateral mechanisms and processes that lack both purposive intent and significant policy bite to manage international order.

The fractured architecture is also a product of the lack of consensus in the region as to how to manage a move away from the post-Cold War status quo. Its many dialogue forums show both an interest in, as well as the weakness of, the institutional vision for regional security order.

Strategic hedging is one way of trying to reconcile these tendencies and manage their implications. But at the heart of the problem lies the fact that Asian countries can't even agree on something twice-removed, namely the need for a consensus (even if only tacit) on the nature and requirements of the regional order in the twenty-first century. Without this, the prospects of a regional security architecture to help protect Asian states and societies in the future are slight.

CHAPTER FOUR

Imagining Alternatives

Increasingly, there are calls in Asia-Pacific for changes in the institutional framework of regional relations. Some, such as Australian Prime Minister Kevin Rudd, have argued for an expansive and ambitious future for Asian multilateralism, whereby a strong centralised institution underwrites an 'Asia-Pacific Community' that maintains regional peace and prosperity.[1] In a similar vein, the newly installed Japanese prime minister, Yukio Hatoyama, put forward his version of an East Asian Community in September 2009 as the best means to achieve regional concord. His view, like Rudd's, took inspiration from Europe and has extensive ambitions, including the adoption of a single currency.[2]

Prominent analysts, such as the Sydney-based Lowy Institute's Allen Gyngell and Jusuf Wanandi from the Centre for Strategic and International Studies (CSIS) in Jakarta, have put forward more modest proposals for rationalising or reorganising the existing range of groupings. This has included calls to scrap the APEC leaders' summit, to create a clearer division of labour between the various regional institutions, and to establish a region-wide body for strategic dialogue that includes all the major powers meeting with genuine and sustained commitment.[3] One particular challenge identified by many analysts and policymakers is to find a better way to accommodate India in regional security mechanisms.

Although these suggestions are less ambitious than efforts to create pan-regional entities, they are still politically challenging, given the considerable diplomatic effort required to bring them about. Such calls show there is a perceived need for the region to create better mechanisms for managing Asia's growing tensions, shared vulnerabilities and conflicts of interest. But as the diversity of ideas also shows, it is not clear how to overcome the obstacles that have so far made the construction of a viable architecture so difficult.

Northeast Asian security mechanism

Given Northeast Asia's longer lack of security institutions it is not surprising that it has been an important contributor to Asia's recent increase in interest in cooperative endeavours. Foremost among these is the possibility that the Six-Party Talks could be transformed into a long-term Northeast Asian security mechanism. The sub-region is also home to the newest Asia-Pacific grouping, the Tripartite Summit of China, Japan and South Korea (see Chapter 2, New dialogue forums).

Scholars such as Columbia University's Samuel Kim have argued that Northeast Asia requires more concerted multi-lateralism, particularly in view of the long-running problems on the Korean peninsula.[4] As China has grown in power and influence, as Northeast Asian states have become more econom-ically integrated, and as the spectre of nuclear proliferation has sharpened security concerns in the region and beyond, Northeast Asian states have turned to multilateral processes.

The Six-Party Talks established in 2003 are at the centre of these efforts. The talks do more than hold out the promise of being able to deal with the more dangerous consequences of North Korea's insecurities. They have also established a viable diplomatic framework, and have garnered sufficient political interest to make possible an ongoing multilateral mechanism to deal with security challenges in this relatively combustible region.

For at least four years, scholars, analysts and diplomats from the United States, Japan and South Korea have been arguing publicly in favour of transforming these talks into a security institution.[5] America's former chief envoy to the talks and assistant secretary of state, Christopher Hill, had this as an important ambition.[6] So, too, did the then secretary of state, Condoleezza Rice.[7]

The Obama administration has indicated that it supports this ambition,[8] an important point of continuity. However, public comment on this has been deliberately low-key, given the desire of officials to get North Korea back to the table after the crises of 2009. All of the parties to the talks are broadly supportive, and the election of the Hatoyama government in 2009 has reduced the influence of Japanese conservatives uneasy about the move.

After North Korea's first nuclear test of October 2006, the talks looked doomed. Yet after intense negotiations between China and the US in December 2006, North Korea was brought back to the table and, under a breakthrough agreement of 13 February 2007, agreed to abide by its September 2005 commitments to denuclearise. The agreement also included the creation of five working groups intended to advance the commitments made under the agreement and to maintain the momentum of the ongoing process.[9]

One working group, chaired by Russia, is responsible for examining the prospects and procedures for creating a 'Northeast Asian Peace and Security Regime'. It is unclear what the parties' concrete plans are for such a body. At the first meeting participants agreed to exclude some sensitive issues, such as Korean reunification, from discussion and matters have not since progressed because of the larger difficulties of the Six-Party process. If it does come about, this 'regime' may begin as a regular contact group, involving sub-ministerial meetings intended to foster dialogue, promote a sense of common cause and establish processes to improve common responses to potential local crises. This may sound a relatively modest ambition. However, given the formal state of war between the two Koreas, the historical animosities among many of the parties, and the latent strategic rivalry among some of the major powers, it would be a considerable achievement.

Obvious immediate benefits would accrue if several of the world's leading powers were to improve their relations through such a group. Beyond this, increased trust and diplomatic goodwill among Russia, China, the US, the Koreas and Japan would have broader pan-regional benefits, especially for Southeast Asian states, which have long recognised that an important determinant of their own security is the state of US–China relations. It could also reduce the uncertainties associated with power transition and reduce the tensions around regional flashpoints. Because of this, many outside Northeast Asia support the move, including the ASEAN states and Australia.[10]

Probably the most important contribution a Northeast Asian security dialogue might make would be to establish a set of procedures to deal with any future sub-regional crises. It is clear that Workers' Party rule in North Korea cannot continue indefinitely, particularly given the rumours around Kim Jong Il's health since late 2008 and the resulting instability in the country. It is uncertain whether the end will come through collapse, negotiated integration with South Korea or through more gradual regime change. In any case, the regional consequences will be dramatic. The geopolitical map of Northeast Asia will be reconfigured, the risk of large population movements will be severe, and the economic implications for South Korea will be tremendous. All of this will require complex diplomatic management, and the framework established by the Six-Party Talks provides an ideal venue for dealing with the international implications of North Korea's end.

A Northeast Asian security regime could also be useful for dealing with future crises across the Taiwan Straits. The 2008 election of Ma Ying-jeou as Taiwan's president has defused some of the tensions that had built up under his predecessor, Chen Shui-bian. However, until there is a final resolution of Taiwan's status, its dispute with Beijing will continue to be a source of serious instability. A Northeast Asian security regime with established procedures could ensure rapid diplomatic response to cross-strait tensions and could be an important means to prevent any crises from spiralling out of control. While it would be unlikely to be able to resolve the broader Taiwanese problem, it would have potential to reduce the damaging international implications of this perennial Asian security challenge.

Other long-term security problems in Northeast Asia where a sub-regional security institution might be of use include Japanese and Chinese military modernisation, and the possibility of an Asian nuclear arms race.[11]

If a regular Northeast Asia grouping were established, it would by no means be certain to avoid the problems faced by existing bodies. To maximise its potential, the body would firstly need to ensure that it maintained a fairly low profile. Part of the reason for the success of the Six-Party Talks has been their relatively small media presence. Candour among diplomats is an important resource, but is in very short supply when the media glare is too bright. To that end, any regular grouping should avoid meeting at too high a level, and should avoid national leaders' summits as a significant part of its programme. That said, national representatives would need to negotiate with authority so that agreements can result in concrete policy commitments. High-level political goodwill is always useful to influence policy choices.

North Korea has proved adept at manipulating the differences in opinion among the five other countries involved in the Six-Party Talks, as well as the gaps between negotiators and their governments. A more institutional form could only operate effectively when such gaps were minimised. Any new body focused on Northeast Asian security would have to find a way to relate to the existing mechanisms, both multilateral and bilateral. Replicating those institutions' lack of coordination and uncertain divisions of labour would significantly limit the efficacy of any new body, and could further reduce the efficiency of regional cooperative efforts.

A Northeast Asian security regime would be of benefit to all of the region's major powers. But how likely is it to come into being? The relative success of the Six-Party Talks provides substantial political capital, which could be invested in creating such a regime. However, heel-dragging by North Korea over many of its commitments throughout the process, and the two nuclear tests of October 2006 and May 2009, has severely dented the prospects for such a move. It is very hard to imagine diplomats being able to institutionalise the talks if North Korea were accepted as a nuclear power. Notwithstanding the talks' relative success, a 2008 study concluded, North Korea would only give up its nuclear ambitions for a very high price.[12] The sorts of concessions it would be likely to extract could be sufficiently high as to scupper ambitions for a Northeast Asian security mechanism.

It may also be that the ideal moment to leverage the success of the talks into an institutional forum has passed, given how far down the nuclear path North Korea has travelled. But the two key powers – China and the US – have maintained a common position toward North Korea, namely that the only diplomatic route open to it is denuclearisation via the Six-Party Talks. This provides a good, if still limited, sign that the complex diplomacy required to turn the framework into something more enduring is still possible.

The institutionalisation of the Six-Party Talks has potential and reasonable support from governments, particularly in South Korea, Japan and the US. However, it will require considerable effort from all the region's major powers if it is to come into being. There are three ways in which the talks might evolve. They could atrophy and ultimately prove ineffective both in resolving the nuclear dispute and in providing a broader diplomatic framework. Secondly, they could remain in place as a contingency-planning body or, thirdly, they could develop into this ongoing mechanism.

The development, or otherwise, of a Northeast Asian security mechanism should be seen as a basic indicator of the broader prospects for security cooperation in the region. If it develops, the chances will be significantly improved that more institutional and cooperative mechanisms can promote international order in Asia; if it does not, it is likely that more power-political mechanisms will continue to predominate. It seems that although the Six-Party Talks are unlikely to disappear altogether, the prospects are slim of their being transformed into something enduring and of policy substance.

ADMM-Plus

Following the relative success of the ASEAN Defence Ministers' Meeting (ADMM) process, ASEAN states have made a formal commitment to creating an ADMM-Plus process comprised of the organisation's dialogue partners and other 'friends of ASEAN'. In February 2009, members at the third ADMM conference adopted the ADMM-Plus concept paper.[13] The group is now intended to meet after ADMM summits and will link intra-ASEAN security cooperation under ADMM auspices with the broader international environment. The first ADMM-Plus is scheduled to be held in Hanoi in 2010.[14] ASEAN is keen to ensure that it remains at the centre of the new process.

However, ADMM-Plus will only come into being if it suits the interests of all ASEAN members, and all potential participants must be approved by all ASEAN countries. It is hoped that the process will complement the ADMM's efforts to improve confidence and transparency among the region's armed forces. Hopefully it will also help to develop an effective platform for joint military action to counter non-traditional security challenges, such as piracy, or to organise disaster relief. For example, ADMM-Plus would be an important adjunct to the humanitarian efforts already being promoted within ASEAN. If it comes into being, and there are reasonable prospects that it will, the ADMM-Plus will add yet another multilateral process to the regional architecture.

It will, however, replicate and overlap with many other regional processes. For example, the defence ministers of all prospective member states already participate in the Shangri-La Dialogue. That said, the grouping has some promise, thanks to ASEAN's commitment to undertake more practical cooperation among the region's armed forces. If successful, ADMM-Plus would make a distinct contribution.

Asian maritime cooperation

Given the shortcomings of pan-regional efforts to foster cooperation and the relative enthusiasm shown toward more concrete and functional forms, there have unsurprisingly been calls to advance a sense of broader trust through more practical cooperative actions. One area in which such collaboration is plainly needed, and where traditional military approaches have proved of limited utility, is maritime security.

Former Indian foreign minister Shiv Shankar Menon has advanced the proposition that security cooperation among Asia's key powers in a 'maritime concert' might be a way in which broader trust among the major powers could develop.[15] The concert could involve all major maritime powers, most particularly China, India and the US, which could collectively clamp down on the non-traditional threats that have thrived in Asia's complex maritime environment, most obviously pirates, criminals and terrorists.

Under the concert, all participating maritime powers would take collective responsibility for the management of specified aspects of the maritime environment. It would also provide a way to manage the maritime friction points where major powers' interests increasingly overlap, such as the Indian Ocean trade routes. As Asian powers grow, the number and sensitivity of these friction points are likely to increase and thus will require careful diplomacy to avoid conflict.

Of course, the problems of leadership and rivalry will beset efforts to establish such a vision of maritime cooperation. However, it does satisfy some of the criteria for cooperative success, namely that it is functionally focused on a concrete question of security concern to all the major powers, it is limited in scope and scale (and not explicitly tied to a *grand projet*) and rests on a foundation of shared interests. If such a regime could be established, there would be a real prospect that it would not only improve the immediate maritime environment but also foster trust among Asia's great powers.

Community building in Asia

Since 2008, there have been three calls for regional community building, distinct from existing efforts within the East Asia Summit (EAS) and the ASEAN Plus Three (APT). Australian PM Kevin Rudd made the first in June 2008, when he set out a vision for an Asia-Pacific Community modelled loosely on the European experience.[16] Rudd argued that Asia needed an all-encompassing institution to drive cooperative efforts across the policy spectrum – a body that included all major powers (China, India, Japan and the US), that was led by national leaders, and that promoted cooperation on economic, strategic and cultural matters.[17] He then despatched retired diplomat Richard Woolcott to canvass regional opinion. Woolcott reportedly met with a fairly equivocal set of responses, although Thailand and Indonesia expressed support for the idea.

At the 2009 Shangri-La Dialogue, Rudd reiterated his vision, while backing away from aspects of the previous year's address.[18] In the 2009 speech, the PM said there was strong regional support for improved cooperation, and a recognition of the shortcomings of existing institutions, especially the absence of a single venue where leaders of all key powers could discuss the full range of policy issues. But he said he had no fixed view on the precise form such a community might take. He conceded there was little appetite for yet another meeting, implying that rationalisation of the existing entities was needed to achieve the Asia-Pacific Community, and said that ASEAN would have a central role to play in the process.

The Australian government held a relatively low-key summit in December 2009 on the possibilities for an Asia-Pacific Community, releasing Woolcott's concept paper beforehand as the starting point for deliberations. The paper fleshes out the key consultation findings, which were highlighted in the Shangri-La Dialogue speech, and proposes that a community could make three contributions to the region, namely that it could:

- help ensure regional prosperity through the promotion of economic openness;
- promote a sense of common strategic cause; and
- help Asia-Pacific states better respond to non-traditional security challenges.[19]

Although there was widespread consensus at the summit on the need for closer ties, there was no agreement on which modalities to pursue. Time will tell how the idea advances.

In September 2009, meanwhile, the newly elected Japanese prime minister, Yukio Hatoyama, set out his own vision for an East Asian community. In an idea first raised in a bilateral meeting with China, he sketched out a body in which the membership would essentially be the same as the APT. He imagined that this community would emanate from the kind of functional cooperation that had led to the formation of the EU, particularly Sino-Japanese cooperation on maritime resource development in the East Asian Sea.[20] This was followed up briefly in his remarks to the UN General Assembly indicating that the construction of the community was a main priority for the 'new' Japan.[21] Foreign Minister Katsuya Okada subsequently indicated that Japan's preferred membership format was that of the broader EAS, including India, Australia and New Zealand alongside the APT states.[22]

While these ideas share several attributes – notably prime ministerial ambition, and a lack of internal and external consultation – they also demonstrate the broader sense in some Asian states that there is a need for institutional change. That is not to say that an Asia-Pacific or an East Asian Community, however conceived, is necessarily something that all agree on. However, there appears to be a perception that there are some basic problems with the region's institutional make-up.

It is interesting that the two states in the region closest to the United States disagree about whether the US should be a part of the community. Australia would seek to incorporate it, but Japan would opt for a narrower vision. This may reflect deeper differences in opinion about trans-Pacific versus East Asian visions of the region. Or it may simply confirm the suspicion that Japan's policy was not fully thought through in advance. Regardless, it shows that even states with closely aligned interests and dependence on American strategic policy can respond to regional prompts in different ways.

While talk of community abounds, there is little support for a strongly institutional vision for the region's architecture. Further, an institution with an all-encompassing political, security and economic agenda may not be appropriate in contemporary Asia. As experience with the ASEAN Regional Forum (ARF) has shown, including more major powers in a group does not necessarily lead to better policy coordination. Looking at APEC, the prospects of wide-ranging economic integration in Asia seem bleak. The 2008 economic crisis is likely to impede integrative efforts, as states will be more inwardly focused and have fewer resources to devote to the task.

That said, the ideas behind the Australian and Japanese calls are widespread. Common economic and strategic interests are drawing Asian states together, but the national structure of decision-making and the sovereign division of authority tends to militate against these interests. At the EAS summit in October 2009, both proposals were presented by their proponents. Although no countries made any firm commitments, China was reportedly more inclined towards the Japanese than the Australian vision. The US is supportive of discussion around community building and the formation of a new mechanism, but it has not committed itself to any particular formation.[23]

Even if a community emerges, it will not have an institutional framework like Europe's. Indeed, any successful multilateral framework for Asia will need to be based on the distinct experiences, interests and values of Asian states. Asian countries have collectively established such bodies in the past – notably ASEAN and the Shanghai Cooperation Organisation (SCO). However, these have been on a much smaller scale, and they displayed more limited policy ambition than either the Japanese or Australian proposals.

Multilateralising the US alliance system

The United States remains the paramount military power in Asia, despite the growing armed might of China and major Asian states. And there appears to be little appetite in Washington for reducing America's regional role, even if the budgetary constraints facing the country in coming years may yet lead to a rethink. At present, the major decision American policymakers face is determining how best to organise the forward projection of power in the region in future. The question is whether American interests are best served through a continuation of the bilateral 'hub-and-spoke' structure or whether a reconfiguration is required. The bilateral structure has some distinct advantages: the US is not subject to more complex alliance politics and can more easily maintain strategic autonomy. However, it also has drawbacks: it is not especially flexible or nimble, and it is of little help in many non-traditional scenarios. It is something of a late-Cold War relic.

One possible way that Asia's security architecture could evolve over the coming years is for the bilateral system to be restructured into a more integrated multilateral system. The primary aim of such a system would be to ensure the geopolitical stability of Asia through a set of guarantees among

alliance members, with military deterrence as the primary stabilising force. The major change to the current order would be
that deterrence was no longer only provided by the US, but by
the full range of alliance partners. This would involve recasting
the basic foundation of Asia's international order away from
its dependence on an exclusively American security guarantee. It would require a commensurate and quite substantial
increase in the military capabilities of alliance partners, notably
Australia, Japan and South Korea.

The logic behind this move, quite apart from reducing the
fiscal and strategic burden on the US, would be to increase
the strategic influence of alliance members, particularly in
their own localities. This would reduce their, and by extension
the region's, dependence on the US, and improve the ability
of the alliance system to contribute to America's broader
global strategy. Over-dependence on the US makes the region
vulnerable to the consequences of American global policy.
When American domestic political opinion favoured a kind of
isolationism in the early 1990s, the region experienced a
collective sense of fear, giving some foretaste of the perils of
over-dependence. The immediate concerns were assuaged
by the Nye reports of 1995 and 1998, in which the US made
a long-term commitment to a substantial forward deployment
of military force in Asia and to the bilateral structure of its
presence there. However, the underlying vulnerability created
by that dependence remained.

America's Asian policy has been affected by its commitments in Afghanistan and Iraq. It has led to a reduction in force
size in Asia, and it has limited the political and strategic flexibility of the broader military presence. While this has only been
of marginal significance to the region's strategic balance, it has
been sufficient to make clear to Asian states the extent to which
they depend on the US. It is in both America's and its Asian

allies' interests to reduce this vulnerability. Multilateralising the alliance system is one way to achieve this.

Such a development would not mean that the region's core security was provided by an institutional system; an underlying logic of power politics would remain central, but it would nonetheless be a more multilateral order. However, transforming the alliance system would be controversial and difficult to achieve. Australia, Japan and South Korea would all have to spend considerably more on defence and, crucially, would need to be much more prepared to use force in their foreign policy.

This would be particularly difficult for Japan, for well-known reasons.[24] The dual challenge of influencing domestic public opinion, both to pay for greater military spending and to change the essence of Japan's security policy, as well as managing the regional concerns that this would provoke would be extremely hard to manage. The ongoing economic problems in Japan and the 2009 election of Hatoyama's Democratic Party of Japan, with its less hawkish foreign and security policy stance, has made this shift even more unlikely. A more militarily powerful Japan, using its might to help underwrite the region's security, would also be difficult for many Asian states to accept, particularly China and South Korea.

Moreover, if the alliance were to continue to have the containment of Chinese military influence as a strategic purpose, it would require Indian participation to be effective. As Professor C. Raja Mohan points out, it may be a mistake to assume that India would never become anyone's ally.[25] Indian policy will be shaped by a sense of its interests, not an ideology of independence. But it seems unlikely that New Delhi's position would change in anything other than a slow and cautious fashion.

The creation of a US-led multilateral alliance structure would almost undoubtedly harden attitudes in China, and probably Russia, towards the US and its partners. It could prompt significant increases in military spending by China and Russia, and would strengthen the argument that they should form a rival alliance. Consequently, regional states would develop more clear-cut strategic affiliations, bringing to an end strategic hedging. Among the more compelling reasons for Asian states to cooperate in their security policy is the sense that most of the more immediate threats to states and societies today come from non-traditional sources. Given that the management of transnational problems requires inclusive security arrangements rather than exclusive alliances, it is hard to see how a multilateralised US alliance system could have an explicit focus on these concerns. Yet without this focus, it would not offer much more to deal with these problems than the current bilateral system does.

In the short term, such a development is unlikely. However, over the medium term one can see some support for it, and small aspects of policy change in this direction are already evident. Australia and Japan have strengthened their alliances with the US and have begun to forge their own formal bilateral security relationship.[26] America is actively courting India and the prospects of a strategic partnership are growing. And there are already American efforts to multilateralise some regional military exercises. The annual *Cobra Gold* exercise began as a joint US–Thai operation, but it has included Singaporean forces since 2000 and involved forces from Japan, the Philippines, Indonesia and other regional states since 2004. The maritime *Cooperation Afloat Readiness and Training* (CARAT) series and the Australian-run biennial *Pitch Black* exercises have also taken on a multilateral character.

However, the greatest single factor limiting the prospects of a US-led multilateral alliance structure remains: namely, the need for partners to spend more on their defence. This is something that most are either unwilling or unable to do.

An Asian security regime?

Another way in which the US alliance system in Asia might evolve would see it transformed into a multilateral mechanism organised around a considerably broader conception of regional security. Such a security regime would perform the traditional function of protecting members from hostile states, but add a wider range of diplomatic and operational dimensions intended to help secure member states and their populations in the face of non-state threats and challenges. This would involve the US alliance system being extended beyond collective defence to provide peacekeeping and humanitarian operations, plus an ability to exert collective diplomatic pressure.

The aim would be to deter states from using aggression to advance their interests, while coordinating regional responses to long-term problems like piracy or acute humanitarian crises emanating from regime collapse or natural disasters. To be effective, it would need to have a permanent headquarters with long-term diplomatic representation from the membership, a secretary general or other leader, and a secretariat to provide support and maintain momentum. NATO's transformation from a traditional collective defence body into a much more flexible entity is one possible template for such an organisation to follow.

Such a body would provide some immediate benefits, beyond the obvious points that it could more effectively manage regional responses to humanitarian problems and other crises. It could also extend support for political change within member states, in the way that NATO has helped buttress the democratisation process in Central and Eastern Europe. Through improved information and communication, it could also be a way of reducing the security dilemmas that arise from processes of military modernisation. It might, for example, be a useful way to reduce regional concern over the transformation of Japan's military and security policy. In short, it could provide a more open foundation for regional stability.

Instead of being organised around an exclusionary logic, the regime could be arranged so it was open to all regional states. By giving a stake in the system to states that might otherwise be concerned about the creation of such a body, it might be possible to reduce the instability that accompanies strategic change.[27] In this way, the participation of both China and India would be possible. Although they might not join, there should be scope for allowing their participation. Perhaps this could be done in the same way the NATO–Russia Council gives Russia regular contact with the Brussels-based body (although the often fraught nature of that relationship, particularly since 2008, warns against putting too much confidence in such a process). Such a body would probably share the inefficiencies that multilateral groups are prone to, particularly in terms of slow decision-making and the dead hand of bureaucratic politics. Participants would have to accept not only higher military spending but also the constraints on their own policy choices that such a body would demand. Given the premium placed on autonomy by many Asian states, initial ambitions for this kind of multilateral grouping might need to be kept modest.

It is hard to envisage such a body coming into being in the near future. The scale of the necessary diplomatic investment would be too high and it would be the kind of institutionally ambitious entity with which Asian states have been uneasy. Importantly, the US does not support the idea, and none of its key regional allies is minded to move in this direction. However, Asia-Pacific states evidently do wish to use both institutional and power-political means to advance their security. Their hedging tendencies could be tapped to support such a regime as it provides both the traditional guarantees of an alliance as well as a host of non-traditional functions.

Flexible coalitions

Overall, Asia-Pacific states do not support institutionally heavy multilateral bodies with wide-ranging agendas. Both the preceding possibilities – a formal 'Community' and an Asian security regime – are hindered by these reservations. But how might the regional mood for more effective regional security cooperation bring about useful endeavours in light of this? One way may be to capitalise on the evident support for functionally specific activity that is not tied to large institution- or order-building projects. This could involve the creation of an institutional framework for cooperative coalitions of interested parties.

It is likely that there will be future regional security problems requiring effective responses from groups of Asian states, from natural disasters in Southeast Asia to state breakdown in North Korea. Interested states could create a body responsible for managing collective responses to regional security problems through cooperative coalitions. Once a particular issue was resolved or managed satisfactorily, the coalition would dissolve, with new ones being forged to deal with subsequent common challenges. As Columbia University scholar Richard Betts argues, we may be familiar with the region's flashpoints, but it is likely that future security crises in Asia will come from unexpected quarters.[28] It is not only North Korea, Kashmir and Taiwan, but possibly Myanmar, Uzbekistan or Mongolia from where crises with regional implications may emerge.

Providing such coalitions are appropriately designed and resourced, this approach could have more flexibility to respond to Asia's geographic diversity effectively than existing institutions. There would need to be a reasonably well-resourced secretariat, perhaps modelled loosely on the UN's Department of Peacekeeping Operations, and its remit would need to be broad. It would have a secretary-general and coordinating staff who 'belonged' to the institution, rather than being seconded from national governments. In the case of the use of force, any coalitions under this arrangement would need to adhere to international law. Such a grouping could take its mandate from Chapter VIII of the UN Charter, which calls for regional solutions to security problems.

By predicating diplomatic and military action on a voluntary basis, and not making it contingent on vetoes or voting, there is a much greater prospect of timely and effective responses to crises. Equally, interaction between members – mostly on matters that do not make major powers feel threatened – could help foster the much sought-after regional sense of common cause. Naturally, such an endeavour would take time to develop. However, a coalition-based cooperative security mechanism has good prospects of providing more effective responses to at least some of the region's security problems. It has also a much greater likelihood of regional support because of its narrow functional ambition. Asia-Pacific states are likely to see it as an attractive proposition.

Other options

Among the wide range of possibilities, several other concepts have been canvassed, even if only briefly. One idea is to create an Asian Security Council. This would involve a region-wide national leaders' summit as the peak forum for security cooperation. At present, there is no single national leaders' group that exclusively discusses security concerns. Such a body could improve confidence and transparency, while coordinating action on non-controversial issues of common concern. One possible drawback is that the mutual mistrust among the major powers would ensure that substantive security concerns were not brought to the table, and that such a body would be confined to superficial issues. Also, unless one of the existing institutions were removed, it would add yet another body competing for the attention of members. Nevertheless, given that it would require a relatively limited diplomatic investment, has modest implications for member states' policies and is focused only on security concerns, it is a distinct possibility. Indeed one prospect being floated in the discussions around a putative Asia-Pacific Community may be for the US to join the EAS and to transform that entity into an Asian Security Council.

A second idea periodically discussed is a Concert of Asia, akin to the post-Napoleonic Concert of Europe first established at the Congress of Vienna in 1815. This idea acknowledges the role played by the great powers in shaping Asia's strategic landscape and would formally recognise it in a diplomatic system managing regional order. Yet, while a directorate of the major powers has an instinctive appeal, it would be impractical because of the kind of coordinated diplomacy a concert requires, as well as the consensus that would be needed among the major powers as to the interests and values the regional order supports.

A third and very recently raised possibility is to create an East Asian caucus of the G20.[29] The G20 has recently become the leading global body for economic policy coordination, and has six East Asian members: Australia, China, Japan, India, Indonesia and South Korea. The intention here would be to use the common economic interests and diplomatic experience of collaboration at the global level to help advance regional cooperative endeavours, such as the EAS or APEC. It could also work to advance a common regional position on global developments, which would in turn have indirect security benefits. This proposal has a practical economic focus but could be harnessed to revitalise institutions, improve regional relations, and promote a more concrete sense of common cause. While a caucus is a real possibility, the APEC experience raises questions as to how technical cooperation on economic matters at a global level could translate into an improved sense of security among Asian states. APEC's logic has been very similar to that of the proposed caucus, but has produced no concrete flow-on security benefits.

The bounds of possibility

There seems to be little short-term prospect of a significant break with current security policy practices in Asia, but what might be possible in the longer term? Asia's present inter-national order is unusual. Since the late 1970s its geopolitical setting has been stabilised by a traditional power-balancing system. In recent years this has been overlain with a range of institutions and dialogue forums variously attempting to forge a new approach to security, to promote an awareness of common interests, and to generally improve the tone and tenor of regional relations. So far, these have made only a fairly superficial impact on state policy choices.

The trends analysed here, however, provide insights into regional thinking about the organisation of international secu-rity – particularly the growing interest in inter-state security cooperation and in the need to revamp aspects of the regional order to reflect new circumstances. If the region has essen-tially been organised on a power-political basis in the past, is an inclusive multilateralism more likely in Asia in the longer-term future?

Trends in the region are pulling in various directions. On the one hand, the convergence of economic interests brought about by rising intra-Asian trade and investment, as well as increasingly shared transnational security threats brought about by globalisation, would appear to favour an order based on multilateral institutions that promote cooperation. On the other hand, nationalism continues to be a powerful force across the region, and the economic prosperity of many Asian states often appears to be strengthening this nationalism. Historical animosity among key powers, the continuing prevalence of balance-of-power thinking in many states, and the broader strategic conservatism in periods of change make wholesale transformation to multilateralism unlikely. Indeed, military procurement trends seem to confirm this hardening of views.

It is hard to avoid the conclusion that, without any significant change in the attitudes of Asian states towards their neighbours and towards institutions, the prospects for inclusive multilateral security cooperation will remain limited. Therefore, the chances of an order in which an 'architecture' plays a prominent role remain slim.

This begs the question: what are the chances of a change in attitude among Asian states? Several factors could increase the possibility of new attitudes towards institutions in the region, including the changing context of Asian states' relations, and shifts within the major powers. Firstly, the increasingly intertwined character of so many states' interests, and the growing perception of a set of threats resistant to traditional security policy approaches, is driving regional demand for cooperation. There is widespread recognition that globalisation is binding Asian states' fates together and it has become a high regional priority to manage the vulnerabilities that these networks create, such as terrorism or infectious disease transmission. Even states that protect their sovereignty jealously recognise that contemporary circumstances may require them to adjust their approach to this principle. ASEAN is also considering policies such as the harmonisation of standards and the adoption of basic-rights principles, which erode traditional approaches to sovereignty.

126 | Building Asia's Security

States are beginning to realise that participating in multilateral institutions may involve bargains that trim elements of state autonomy. However, they also realise that such bargains do not necessarily compromise national independence and that they can manage the political consequences.[30] Thus, the changing character of Asian states' interests, their perception of their security environment, and a gradual lowering of the barrier of traditional 'sovereignty absolutism' may have all improved the prospects for a more effective form of security cooperation.

However, a broader convergence of interests in favour of cooperation is not sufficient on its own. In Asia, the prospects for security cooperation rely most crucially on the attitudes of the major powers. How China, India, the US and, to a lesser extent, Japan approach security cooperation is the single most important factor likely to affect the future of Asia-Pacific security cooperation.

The stagnation of the ARF since 2003 has been due largely to the strategic ambivalence of the major powers, particularly the US, towards the grouping. No amount of tinkering with institutional design, working out more efficient divisions of labour between APEC, the ARF and the EAS, or devising new structures will make much difference if the major powers are not especially interested. Indeed, as a 2009 essay on the prospects of a regional security architecture observed, the most important development stabilising Asia's international order in the past 60 years occurred through the 1970s normalisation of Sino-American relations. This is a salutary reminder of the importance of great-power relations for the region's security.[31]

Are there signs that the major powers' attitudes towards security cooperation specifically, and regional institutions more generally, are likely to be more conducive to success in the future than they have been since the 1990s? American lack of enthusiasm for multilateral security institutions in Asia is well known; the US is deeply committed to the bilateral alliance system. But there are signs that Washington realises the need to change the political and diplomatic dimensions of its Asian policy. The shifting approach toward the Six-Party Talks, and more particularly the push to regularise these into a Northeast Asian framework under the last Bush administration, is one sign of this trend. The Obama administration also supports cooperative measures and is well disposed towards institutional approaches to order in Asia. The new administration is slightly more inclined to see value in habits of security cooperation and dialogue processes for their own sake than its predecessor. Nevertheless, the indications are that the US will continue a pragmatic approach to security institutions, especially if one heeds comments by Assistant Secretary of State Kurt Campbell.[32] Cooperation will need to provide real benefits and significant progress, and failure to move beyond current practices would make the US an aloof, if not absent, partner.

The possibility that China and India may take a more sympathetic view of regional institutions has also increased since 2003–04. Neither is set to become the champion of a strongly institutionalised international order. However, each country's economic circumstances, and their shared wish not to see the region dominated by the US, may more favourably dispose them towards security institutions than in the past. Both rely on stable geopolitical circumstances to fuel domestic economic development, which in turn is necessary for domestic political stability. China and India also seek to be leading players in regional affairs. Taking a diplomatic leadership role in any new institutional order may satisfy this ambition and serve their interests by providing opportunities to shape institutional structures in their favour.

China and India have both become active, pragmatic and efficient diplomatic players. They have the capacity and skills necessary to encourage the growth of multilateralism. Moreover, each of them feels that a continuation of power politics or a revival of containment is not to its advantage.[33] Although they may have a common interest in avoiding the worst features of power-political systems, such as destabilising arms races, geopolitical instability and increased defence expenditure, it does not follow that they would automatically work together. China and India are hardly natural collaborators and it would require considerable movement for them to work in such a fashion. However, improved cooperation does not depend only on their joint leadership. One or both of these rising powers could spark a change in attitude among the major powers that would enable security institutions to exert a more significant influence on the region's order.

Finally, ASEAN is no longer at the heart of all regional cooperative endeavours. This alone may increase the prospects for more substantive cooperation, as the institutional handbrake of the 'ASEAN way' is increasingly released. Of course, Asian states could find other reasons not to make cooperation substantive. However, the changing nature of Asian states' interests, the shifting attitudes of key powers, and a greater appreciation of the need for more concrete security cooperation all indicate that efforts to foster some kind of regional architecture may have more purchase in the future.

Asia is moving from a stable international order towards a hybrid system where elements of the old order remain, hints of the new are visible and uncertainty abounds. Cooperative mechanisms are playing an important, but so far relatively minor, part in this process. However, they hold out considerable promise to help manage the transition. At the sub-regional level, cooperation can help resolve specific crises and defuse tensions both current, such as territorial disputes in the South China Sea, or future, such as a collapse of the regime in North Korea. They can promote better policies for dealing with non-traditional security and help improve responses to humanitarian catastrophe, both natural and human-induced.

In the larger regional picture, multilateral mechanisms could help foster a stable order as power becomes more widely distributed across the region and as states' interests become more closely intertwined. Multilateral bodies can reduce the strategic uncertainties of periods of power transition. Yet the realisation of a regional security architecture remains a distant ideal. The limitations imposed by bureaucratic underinvestment, by cautious states wary of one another, by the shortage of leadership and by Asian states' widely varying perceptions of the basic security challenges they face have all hampered – and are likely to continue to hamper – the development of a more integrated security system that fosters a stable regional order.

Ways Forward

Asia's economic transformation is improving lives across the region and is knitting together the fates of disparate societies. However, this growing connectivity and increased interdependence is not automatically harmonising Asian states' security interests. Strategic uncertainty caused by both China and India's growing power and international confidence, by Japan's military modernisation and by the United States' preoccupation with Iraq and Afghanistan is leading Asian states to increase their defence expenditure. Asian nations are increasingly aware of the problems caused by globalisation, such as transnational crime, energy dependence, food insecurity and infectious diseases; governments realise that they need new approaches to these problems to secure their interests. In response to these twin developments – geostrategic uncertainty and new transnational threats – Asian states have increasingly involved themselves in diverse forms of security cooperation.

The region now has an extensive range of mechanisms, processes and dialogue forums – of various degrees of institutionalisation – which cover everything from anti-piracy patrols in the Malacca Straits to counter-terrorism exercises in Central

Asia. Despite strong regional interest in greater multilateralism and many different visions of an Asian security architecture, the achievements of Asia's cooperative efforts to date have been modest. The tensions that exist between economic integration and geostrategic uncertainty are leading countries to hedge their approach to security policy, and this is evident in the ongoing shortcomings of so many cooperative efforts. Without significant shifts in attitude from individual countries, the current flurry of security multilateralism is unlikely to recast the regional order.

That the strong interest in cooperation has not led to more effective measures or better institutions is clear. It is also plain that there is little chance that a pan-Asian security architecture similar to Europe's will emerge in the short to medium term. There are several important reasons why efforts to drive security cooperation forward seem at present unable to capitalise on the evident regional interest. The most obvious of these lies in Asia's uncertain geopolitical circumstances. Realists have long argued that the structure of the international system predisposes states to be sceptical of cooperation's worth. This predisposition has been exacerbated by the shifts in power caused by China's resurgence and India's rise. It is not that Asian states fear the aggression of either of these new powers, but rather that their growth has produced a sense of destabilisation – an unusual experience given America's generation-long strategic dominance.

The shortcomings of the cooperative bodies themselves make up the second inhibiting factor. Many are hindered by a preference for process over policy, an inability to move beyond superficial aspects and cumbersome decision-making. In some cases, such as the ASEAN Regional Forum (ARF), there are evident differences among members as to what the institution is for. A larger problem is that various powers in the region have quite divergent views as to the sources of insecurity that they face. Thus, reaching consensus on appropriate common policies for mitigating these insecurities is, in many cases, almost impossible. Collaborative efforts are also seriously undermined by the lack of coordination among bodies, which disperses and dilutes scarce diplomatic resources. This also creates inefficient diplomatic processes where, for example, almost the same group of states meets at both the East Asia Summit (EAS) and the ARF to talk about often similar issues to little obvious benefit.

A third reason for failure is significant diplomatic and bureaucratic underinvestment. While most Asian states espouse a cooperative and multilateral rhetoric, none matches it with fiscal investment. This is a self-perpetuating problem. Underinvestment in cooperative mechanisms means they are less able to make progress in advancing common security goals, which leads participating states to feel that it is not worth investing more, because of institutional underachievement.

The final problem derives from great-power indifference to cooperation. While the major powers are part of most cooperative efforts, they have shown little genuine enthusiasm for collaboration on security matters. The competitive tensions evident in some multilateral efforts, such as the EAS, or tensions between groupings like the ASEAN Plus Three (APT) and EAS, are largely due to the longer-running mutual mistrust and nascent rivalry of Asia's major powers.

It is tempting, therefore, to conclude that multilateral security cooperation in Asia will continue to be of only marginal influence in the region. Perhaps it could be useful in better coordinating disaster relief or dealing with uncontroversial humanitarian operations, but it would appear to have little chance of mitigating the region's more complex security challenges and almost no prospect of underwriting the region's international order in the long term. But while there is little appetite for a rigid and centrally organised institution, there is interest in the ability of cooperative elements of the region's fractured architecture to reduce strategic uncertainties, improve policy coordination in uncontroversial areas, and to help deal with common non-traditional challenges. Beyond taking comfort from the fact that Europe's multifaceted architecture took more than 50 years, and the small matter of the Cold War, to emerge, those who aspire to a more institutional or architectural basis for Asia's regional security order should not be too disheartened by contemporary circumstances.

Building on existing benefits

Despite their apparent shortcomings, cooperative efforts already contribute in important ways to regional stability. The Six-Party Talks have been instrumental in defusing tensions in the Korean Peninsula. Even if they ultimately fail to denuclearise North Korea, the talks have shown the utility of multilateral mechanisms to help manage security crises. They have also proved that the US and China can work together effectively under a multilateral umbrella. Elements of the fractured architecture have played an important part in helping to manage China's emergence as a major regional power, in the face of considerable apprehension. Despite their limitations, the Malacca Strait Patrols have helped to reduce security risks in one of the region's most crucial waterways. They have also demonstrated the efficacy of specific functional mechanisms.

Without the current architecture, despite its flaws, contemporary regional security circumstances would be much less stable and predictable. It is also clear that the region's multilateral groupings are valued, albeit to varying degrees, by most Asian states. Having regular venues for diplomatic exchanges, particularly at ministerial level, is seen as particularly useful.

The enthusiasm for the Asian Defence Ministers' Meeting (ADMM) and the Shangri-La Dialogue is evidence of this. Most countries recognise that the basic habits of multi-lateral cooperation and dialogue are of considerable utility and worth retaining. This is so, even if they do not agree about the extent to which such processes should shape the broader contours of regional order, or about the degree to which institutional commitment should constrain their policy choices.

Regional demand for multilateral security approaches ultimately derives from the following realisation: that ongoing peace and stability in Asia will depend on how Asian states manage the inevitable clashes of interest that emerge as the distribution of power changes. That some kind of cooperative framework is needed is clear. Thus, collaborative security mechanisms of varying kinds will play a part in Asia's future. The challenge lies in developing measures that both lead to concrete cooperative action in managing these challenges more effectively and that bolster the sense of security felt by states and peoples. At present, the ad hoc interaction of various multilateral and bilateral processes forms a partial architecture. It stabilises aspects of the region's international relations, but it does so only in a limited and uneven fashion.

In response to the broader perception that the region's security challenges require improved multilateralism, and to address the manifest shortcomings of today's fractured architecture, ambitious politicians like the Australian and Japanese prime ministers, as well as concerned scholars and analysts, have called for a more effective regional architecture – one that is better equipped to reduce strategic uncertainties and facilitate common action in response to shared risks.

So how can those who wish to build a better security architecture for Asia learn from the present shortcomings?

Towards a networked approach

From an institutional point of view, the greatest promise for regional security cooperation comes from linking a pan-regional, high-level forum with a series of functionally specific efforts organised on a sub-regional basis. Two such possible high-level forums might be a Southeast Asian maritime security agency or a Northeast Asian crisis-response mechanism.

It is often assumed that a single, coherent and tightly organised architecture offers the best prospects for regional security. The challenge is thought to lie in working out how to get to it from today's tangled web, and there are quite varied perspectives on the best route. One approach might be to build the edifice incrementally, sub-region by sub-region, eventually linking all the elements. Another view is for a grand, top-down design.

But the assumption about the goal may be misplaced. Rather, it is entirely possible that the region can be made more secure through a complex and relatively loosely organised security architecture. There is no requirement for a single European-style approach to secure Asian states and societies. This is not to defend the status quo; the current fractured architecture is clearly unsatisfactory. But it is a false choice to think it necessary either to build a massive multilateral edifice or be forever condemned to the vagaries of the balance of power. The immediate need is for more creative thinking about the role that cooperation plays in Asia's emerging international order.

Assuming that the regional demand for multilateral security cooperation is real and likely to endure, and that the major problems lie on the supply side, it is reasonable to conclude that there may be a more basic problem with institutions as a means to achieving the cooperative goal. Clearly, some of the existing institutional mechanisms have particular problems that limit their effectiveness. The weaknesses of ASEAN and the Asia

Pacific Economic Cooperation (APEC) forum, for example, are widely recognised. However, the repeated difficulty in turning regional interest in cooperation into increased confidence and security through institutional means should prompt a rethink of the underlying edifice: perhaps international institutions, as traditionally understood, are not the best way to improve the security setting of Asia's states and peoples?

Institutions are unsuitable not only because of Asian states' reluctance to endow them with any significant policy capacity, or because of general scepticism about institutional bureaucracy and inefficiency. The geographic and functional diversity of security problems across Asia would test even the best-resourced institution. What is required to ameliorate geopolitical uncertainty and territorial disputes among states in Northeast Asia is almost entirely different from what is required to respond to infectious-disease transmission in maritime Southeast Asia.

While international institutions may be an instinctive framework that policymakers and analysts turn to when trying to devise ways of cooperating, the capacity of institutions in Asia (and indeed elsewhere) to cope with contemporary circumstances seems to be increasingly in question. Many global institutions are hamstrung by outdated structures, mandates and membership, including the UN Security Council and the IMF. But formal international institutions themselves have an anachronistic quality.

Groupings of states organised on the basis of formal equality meeting to advance commonly held goals made sense after 1945. They were the only means for states to deal with common problems. Over the past 60 years, however, the explosion in the number of new states, the dramatic increase in the speed with which goods, money and ideas can travel, changes to the way in which sovereignty is understood and the increasingly porous nature of borders have all meant that this approach to solving common problems is increasingly of limited utility.

As such, no amount of careful institutional design or dramatically increased bureaucratic investment will produce much in terms of security benefits. The distinctive problems and challenges of Asia's rapidly evolving security landscape insist on new approaches to security cooperation.

Several scholars have begun to make the case that the connectivity of contemporary world politics means that many key policy goals can only be achieved through transnational networks.[1] In this view, states will need to do more than work in coordination with other states and international organisations; they must also cooperate with non-state actors, such as civil-society organisations, companies and other bodies that operate below state level, as well as transnationally. Some countries, such as Australia and the UK, actively engage non-state actors to help advance their climate-change policies, by mobilising civil-society organisations to promote awareness and action, as well as integrating private firms into emission-trading schemes.

Asian states and societies could advance much-needed security collaboration through a network of cooperative security nodes, rather than a formal structure of inter-state institutions. The aim would be to create a series of linkages between centres of influence and power, to manage security-related problems. These nodes may be more traditional inter-state mechanisms, such as the Six-Party Talks. However, in others they might involve transnational connections between states, private security firms, civil-society organisations and multinational enterprises.

Private security firms are playing an increasingly important role in security and strategic policy across the world.[2] Two examples of this trend in Asia include the use of private firms to support UN military police in Timor Leste (East Timor) and the hiring of private security firms as armed escorts to private shipping clients in the Malacca Straits.[3] While this latter case has caused some unease among the littoral states, Indonesia and Malaysia, a working accommodation has been reached among at least some of these private actors, which indicates one way in which a more networked approach may develop.[4]

Security networks would be functionally specific, forged to achieve specific tasks and dissolved when the task was complete. They could also be easily reconfigured if initially unable to achieve their goal. The advantage of a networked approach to security cooperation is its speed, flexibility and fluidity. The challenge for Asian states is to determine how to lay down the diplomatic and policy infrastructure of such a network without compromising its organic and bottom-up attributes – for it is precisely these qualities that make a network approach effective. To some extent, Asia's early forays into Track II diplomacy represented an embryonic networked approach.

A networked approach to security cooperation is, in some respects, merely catching up with the realities of a globalising international system. As the networks of transnational terrorism, criminality and economic-production systems show, not only are such actors able to thrive in these conditions, they are also able to elude or outpace state efforts to control, contain or regulate their activities. Equally, the dense and shifting populations of Asia are vulnerable to the rapid spread of infectious diseases. In a pandemic, it would require not just strict quarantine efforts but the effective marshalling of civil-society organisations, firms and state entities to devise and develop vaccines, distribute medicines and ensure hygienic practice in a timely fashion. Asian security policymakers must recognise this feature of the new security landscape and adjust their aspirations accordingly.

Tidying the clutter

A networked approach does not preclude international institutions; indeed, they will be important nodes in such a system. But an immediate challenge is to deal with Asia's institutional clutter. The region has too many bodies associated with security cooperation. Bureaucratic resources are spread too thinly, the opportunities for obfuscation are too great, and the inefficiencies of overlap badly diminish the policy efficacy of these efforts.

A vital step in reforming the current setting is to create a division of labour among the groupings, one that is related both to membership and policy coverage. The APEC leaders' summit could be reformulated as an Asian Council, which would meet annually to discuss matters of common concern across all policy spheres. The region might also benefit from a clearer-cut sub-regional division of labour. The EAS might act as an umbrella organisation for smaller sub-regional entities, for example, a successor to the Six-Party Talks in Northeast Asia and the ADMM operating in Southeast Asia.

These are just some of the possibilities. Whatever emerges, Asian states need to stop adding to the institutional clutter, and to devise a more effective distribution of work among the entities. In so doing, they should recognise the frictions between bilateralism and multilateralism. At the very least, plans should be laid out for better managing the interaction between bilateral and multilateral processes. Otherwise, the risk remains that bilateral and competitive approaches could overwhelm the multilateral and cooperative.

The prospects for more effective cooperation would appear to be greater through the reform of existing entities – because these have extant organisational structures, as well as political and diplomatic leverage – rather than through the creation of bodies *de novo*. That said, the ill-will towards, and the bad public reputation of, some groupings may contradict this broader point. It might therefore be time to consider whether all of the existing entities in Asia deserve continued support. For example, without a significantly better division of labour among them, it is not especially helpful to persist with all three of APEC, the APT and the EAS. There are only so many summits and meetings that can be attended while still generating useful policy outcomes.

Satisfying the basic regional requirement for more cooperation will require greater diplomatic and bureaucratic investment. The levels of trust and sense of shared interests among the major powers need to increase if a more effective security architecture or broader-ranging sense of community is to be possible. This would need to begin with major powers wishing to improve coordination and hence seeking to build trust. From there, specific efforts to advance this would need to be pursued, such as bilateral dialogues at senior official and ministerial level to identify areas of common concern and shared risk. On top of these, a platform for more effective broader collaboration could be built. The tendency in the region to see confidence building as an end in itself – and therefore as a useful way to avoiding more concrete moves – must be recognised.

All of this will require a substantial change in the attitudes of the major powers; this in turn will only come about with changes in the way major powers conceive of their interests. This is by no means an inevitable result, but greater levels of cooperation will require such a transformation – one that essentially must be led by shifts in the domestic political and policy framework of Asia's major powers. These powers must also all be included in any broader-ranging regional edifice, of whatever institutional weight. Exclusion of any major power, particularly the US, would be counterproductive.

Seizing the opportunity

The creation of a security architecture will require time, investment and, most crucially, policy creativity by the participating
states. Those who support the construction of a regional security architecture must convince Asian states that they should
invest more time and money in cooperative endeavours.
Cooperation is a slow and expensive process, and one that has
suffered from chronic underinvestment. Supporters of cooperation must match their ambitions with resources. The economic
difficulties of 2008–09, and their longer-term implications for
so many in Asia, will make this particularly challenging.

Asian states will also need to improve their diplomatic
handling of security cooperation. Multilateral processes are
naturally cumbersome and prone to loss of momentum and
distraction. Careful attention must be paid to this tendency,
and willing states will need to provide leadership whenever
interest in cooperative endeavours flags. Without diplomatic
leadership, as well as new ideas and an appropriate budgetary
allowance to pursue them, cooperation on security matters in
Asia may not advance significantly.

While institutions have clear limitations, a security architecture that brings networks of security mechanisms holds out
considerable promise for the region. This is not just because it
can help to reassure insecure states, reduce the chances of military escalation through improved information flows, and foster
a sense of common cause among diverse states. It can also be a
way of formally recognising the changing power dynamic and
the legitimacy of the claims of new powers.

Historically, emerging powers have often felt belittled by
existing international structures and complained of not being
given appropriate recognition of their new status. The sense
that there is insufficient respect for a state's international standing can be grist to the mill of radical nationalist groups. Stable

international systems are built not only on balanced distributions of power, but also on mutual respect for the status and legitimacy of powers. It is vital that Asia's security architects use the mood for international cooperation to recognise the political legitimacy and status of emerging powers. They need to entrench that recognition in the foundations of a new regional order.

There are presently two divergent trends in Asia's changing strategic landscape. On the one hand, economic linkages are fostering increased interdependence, and globalisation is making plain the shared vulnerabilities of Asian states. This should be an environment extremely conducive to multilateral cooperation. On the other hand, the changing power distribution, uncertainty and perceptions of risk are generating security dilemmas, which are magnified by pervasive nationalism. The region has produced a fractured security architecture that reflects these divergent trends. This hybrid international order has both institutional and power-political features, but the latter still predominate.

There is a genuine prospect of a move away from a power-political system towards one in which cooperative features, whether networked or institutional, play a greater role. However, such a move will be difficult to achieve. There is a realisation in the region that structural change is under way, and it is clear that the post-Cold War strategic status quo cannot continue indefinitely. The moment is, as Singaporean diplomat Kishore Mahbubani puts it, quite 'plastic'.[5] The years between 2010 and 2020, therefore, will befundamentally important in establishing the parameters of Asia's new international order. There is thus an ideal opportunity to create more cooperative security mechanisms that can better meet the needs of all of Asia's states and societies. To build Asia's security through the improvement of the region's currently fractured architecture will ultimately be a question of political will. Key states are setting out competing visions as to how this might be advanced, and while the present circumstances are extremely conducive to increasing concrete security cooperation, this is by no means automatically going to occur.

The extent to which states in the region capitalise on this opportunity depends on how they respond to changing circumstances. In China and India's recent diplomacy one sees some signs of change. A more multilateral-friendly US also augurs well for the prospects of security multilateralism. It is in America's interest to play a central role in the efforts to reshape regional order. American ambition to retain a leadership role in Asia should also give succour to those who support regional security cooperation.

That said, one should not underestimate either the difficulties of creating a more effective institutional structure or the time that this will take to achieve. Asia's material circumstances could hardly be better placed to foster an effective security architecture. However, the political environment does not seem as advantageous. And it is at that level that most work needs to be done to make Asia's states and societies more secure.

GLOSSARY

ADMM	ASEAN Defence Ministers' Meeting
APEC	Asia Pacific Economic Cooperation
APSC	ASEAN Political-Security Community
APT	ASEAN Plus Three
ARF	ASEAN Regional Forum
ARF/VDR	ARF's Voluntary Demonstration of Response on Disaster Relief
ASEAN	Association of Southeast Asian Nations
ASEAN–ISIS	ASEAN–Institutes for Strategic and International Studies
EAS	East Asia Summit
CEAC	Council for East Asian Community
CFSP	Common Foreign and Security Policy
CMI	Chiang Mai Initiative
CSCAP	Council for Security and Cooperation in the Asia-Pacific
CTTF	Counter-Terrorism Task Force
ESDP	European Security and Defence Policy
EU	European Union
FPDA	Five Power Defence Arrangements
IISS	The International Institute for Strategic Studies
MSP	Malacca Strait Patrols
NATO	North Atlantic Treaty Organisation
NEAT	Network of East-Asian Think Tanks

OPEC	Organisation of Petroleum Exporting Countries
OSCE	Organisation for Security and Cooperation in Europe
PECC	Pacific Economic Cooperation Council
PSI	Proliferation Security Initiative
RCTS	Regional Counter-Terrorist Structure
SCO	Shanghai Cooperation Organisation
SEATO	Southeast Asia Treaty Organisation
SAARC	South Asian Association for Regional Cooperation
SARS	Severe Acute Respiratory Syndrome
STAR	Secure Trade in the Asia-Pacific Region
TAC	Treaty of Amity and Cooperation in Southeast Asia
TSD	Trilateral Strategic Dialogue
UN	United Nations
UNSC	United Nations Security Council
WMD	Weapons of Mass Destruction
ZOPFAN	Zone of Peace, Freedom and Neutrality

NOTES

Introduction

1. Kevin Rudd, Address to the Asia Pacific community conference Sydney, 4 December 2009, http://www.pm.gov.au/node/6368.

2. Richard Woolcott talking to Linda Mottram in 'Conference to promote Rudd's Asia Pacific community', ABC Radio Australia, 3 December 2009, http://www.radioaustralia.net.au/connectasia/stories/200912/s2760878.htm.

3. Kishore Mahbubani, *The New Asian Hemisphere: The Irresistible Shift of Global Power to the East* (New York: Public Affairs, 2008).

4. Kevin Rudd talking to Jim Middleton, 'Australia promotes Asia Pacific community plan', ABC Radio Australia, 4 December 2009, http://www.radioaustralia.net.au/connectasia/stories/200912/s2762004.htm.

5. Bill Emmott, *Rivals: How the Power Struggle Between China, India and Japan Will Shape our Next Decade* (London: Allen Lane, 2008.)

6. 'Clashes on Thai-Cambodian border', BBC News, 3 April 2009, http://news.bbc.co.uk/1/hi/world/asia-pacific/7980535.stm.

7. Thom Shanker and Mark Mazzetti, 'China and U.S. clash on Naval Fracas', *The New York Times*, 10 March 2009, http://www.nytimes.com/2009/03/11/world/asia/11military.html?_r=1.

8. IISS, *The Military Balance, 2009* (London: Routledge, 2009), pp. 363–424, see particularly pp. 372–76.

9. See for example, Tony Hotland, 'Differences hinder Asia-Pacific bloc', *Jakarta Post*, 6 June 2008; Hugh White, 'The Asia Pacific Community concept: right task, wrong tool?', 26 April 2009, http://www.eastasiaforum.org; and Daniel Flitton, 'Minister spurns PM's region idea', *The Age*, 19 November 2009, http://www.theage.com.au/national/minister-spurns-pms-region-idea-20091118-imle.html.

10. SEATO was a collective defence organisation founded in 1954. Although planned as an Asian version of NATO, it lacked that organisation's unified military command structures, and members were not obliged to respond if a member state were attacked. Instead, a unanimous vote was required to sanction collective action, leaving

individual member states able with a veto. Countries gradually lost interest and SEATO was formally disbanded in the 1970s.

11 On this see Christopher Hemmer and Peter J. Katzenstein, 'Why is there no NATO in Asia? Collective Identity, Regionalism and Multilateralism', *International Organization* vol. 56, no. 3, 2002, pp. 575-607.

12 Allan Gyngell, 'Design Faults: The Asia-Pacific's Regional Architecture' *Lowy Institute Policy Brief* (Sydney: Lowy Institute for International Policy, 2007).

13 'Hatoyama pushes East Asian community', *Asahi Shimbun* 23 September, 2009, http://www.asahi.com/english/Herald-asahi/TKY200909230045.html.

Chapter One

1 Charles L. Glaser, 'Realists as Optimists: Cooperation as Self-help', *International Security*, vol. 19, no. 1, 1994–95, pp. 50–40.

2 This can be seen in the recent security cooperation dimensions of the Southern African Development Community which give the appearance of strong commitments but in reality have little policy substance behind them. See Anne Hammerstad, *Defending the State or Protecting the People? SADC Security Integration at a Crossroads* SAIIA Report No. 39, (Johannesburg: SAIIA, 2003).

3 For example see Amitav Acharya, 'Regional Institutions and Security in the Asia-Pacific: Evolution, Adaptation and Prospects for Transformation' in Amitav Acharya and Evelyn Goh (eds), *Reassessing Security Cooperation in the Asia-Pacific: Competition, Congruence and Transformation* (Cambridge, MA: MIT Press, 2007), pp. 19–40; particularly pp. 20–5.

4 On the distinction between competitive and cooperative forms of collaboration generally, see William T. Tow, *Tangled Webs: Security Architectures in Asia* (Canberra: Australian Strategic Policy Institute, 2008) http://www.aspi.org.au/publications/publication_details.aspx?ContentID=174&pubtype=0.

5 On this generally, see William T. Tow, 'Asia's Competitive "Strategic Geometries": The Australian Perspective', *Contemporary Southeast Asia,* vol. 30, no. 1, 2008, pp. 29–51.

6 See generally, Robert D. Blackwill and Paul Dibb (eds), *America's Asian Alliances* (Cambridge, MA: MIT Press, 2000).

7 See Bates Gill, Michael Green, Kiyoto Tsuji and William Watts, *Strategic View on Asian Regionalism: Survey Results and Analysis* (Washington, DC: Center for Strategic and International Studies, 2009).

8 On this more generally, see Nick Bisley, *Rethinking Globalization* (Basingstoke: Palgrave Macmillan, 2007).

9 On the structural implications of changing power configurations, see Coral Bell, *The End of the Vasco da Gama Era: The Next Landscape of World Politics* (Sydney: Lowy institute for International Policy, 2007).

10 See generally Brendan Taylor, 'Security Cooperation in the Asia-Pacific Region' in Ron Huisken and Meredith Taylor (eds), *History as Policy: Framing the Debate on the Future of Australian Defence Policy* (Canberra: ANU E-Press, 2007) pp. 117–28.

11 Robert O. Keohane, Helga Haftendorn and Celeste Wallander, 'Introduction', in their (eds), *Imperfect Unions: Security Institutions Over Time* (Oxford: Clarendon Press, 1999), pp. 1–18; pp. 1–2; see also Hedley Bull, *The Anarchical Society: A Study of Order in World Politics* (Basingstoke: Macmillan, 1985), p. 71. In Bull's definition, they are not simply administrative machinery but 'a set of habits and practices shaped toward the realisation of common goals'.

12 Robert Ayson and Brendan Taylor, 'Architecture alternatives or alternatives to architecture' in Ron Huisken, *Rising China: Power and Reassurance* (Canberra: ANU E-Press, 2009) Chapter 13, Section 2 http://epress.anu.edu.au/sdsc/rc/mobile_devices/ch14s02.html.

13 On cooperative security in Asia see Amitav Acharya, *Regionalism and Multilateralism: Essays on Cooperative Security in the Asia-Pacific* (Singapore: Times academic Press, 2002); on security community see Emanuel Adler and Michael Barnett (eds), *Security Communities* (Cambridge: Cambridge University Press, 1998).

14 See William T. Tow and Brendan Taylor, 'Challenges to Building an Effective Asia-Pacific Security Architecture' in Michael J. Green and Bates Gill (eds), *Asia's New Multilateralism: Cooperation, Competition and the Search for Community* (New York: Columbia University Press, 2009), pp. 454–87; p. 458–9.

15 For example, Barry J. Eichengreen, *Toward a New International Financial Architecture: A Practical Post-Asia Agenda* (Washington, DC: Institute for International Economics, 1999); and Il Sakong and Yunjong Wang (eds), *Reforming the International Financial Architecture: Emerging Market Perspectives* (Seoul: Korea Institute for International Economic Policy, 2000).

16 For example, see Alan Dupont, 'New Dimensions of Security' in Denny Roy (ed.), *The New Security Agenda in the Asia-Pacific* (Basingstoke: Macmillan, 1997). For an overview of the arguments from this period see Craig A. Snyder (ed), *Contemporary Security and Strategy* (Basingstoke: Macmillan, 1999).

17 For an example of this, see the 2003 Australian foreign policy white paper which made clear that the then Australian government felt that new security challenges of terrorism, unregulated population flows, weak states, transnational crime and infectious diseases were the pre-eminent challenge. See *Advancing the National Interest* (Canberra: Commonwealth of Australia, 2003), http://australianpolitics.com/foreign/elements/2003_whitepaper.pdf.

18 See Paul Cornish, 'NATO: the practice and politics of transformation', *International Affairs*, vol. 80, no. 1, 2004, pp. 63–74.

19 See Anthony Forster and William Wallace, 'What is NATO for?', *Survival*, vol. 43, no. 4, 2002, pp. 107–22.

20 On this see Mark Webber, Stuart Croft, Jolyon Howorth, Terry Terriff and Elke Krahmann, 'The governance of European security', *Review of International Studies*, vol. 30, no. 1, 2004, pp. 3–26.

21 On ESDP, see Jolyon Howorth, *European Integration and Defence:*

The Ultimate Challenge?, WEU–IIS, Chaillot Paper No. 43, 2000, especially Chapter 2, http://www.iss.europa.eu/publications/chaillot-papers/#c893.

22 On this, see Celeste A. Wallander and Robert O. Keohane, 'Risk, Threat and Security Institutions' in Robert O. Keohane, Helga Haftendorn and Celeste Wallander (eds), *Imperfect Unions*, pp. 26-9.

23 See Javier Solana, *A Secure Europe in a Better World: European Security Strategy* (Brussels: 2003). In December 2007, the Council requested that the High Representative revisit the strategy. At the time of writing, there has been no new statement.

24 Council meetings were suspended in September 2008 after the Georgian conflict but restarted in December 2008.

25 Robert Ayson and Brendan Taylor, 'Architecture alternatives or alternatives to architecture' in Ron Huisken, *Rising China: Power and Reassurance* (Canberra: ANU E-Press, 2009), Chapter 13, Section 2, http://epress.anu.edu.au/sdsc/rc/mobile_devices/ch14s02.html.

26 For example, see the reported remarks of the Singaporean Defence Minister at the 2008 IISS Shangri-La Dialogue, 'Modes of Security Cooperation: Confidence Building, partnerships, alliances', Chapter Nine of the *Shangri-La Dialogue Report 2008*, http://www.iiss.org/publications/conference-proceedings/shangri-la-dialogue-report-2008/plenary-session-6/.

Chapter Two

1 See Amitav Acharya, *Constructing a Security Community in Southeast Asia: ASEAN and the Problem of Regional Order* (London: Routledge, 2000).

2 Japan Center for International Exchange, 'Track I: Governmental Meetings', *Dialogue and Research Monitor: Inventory of Multilateral Meetings on Asia Pacific Security and Community Building*, http://www.jcie.or.jp/drm/2007/track1.html. Some of the meetings listed cover largely economic cooperation, but the vast bulk are focused on security matters.

3 William T. Tow and Brendan Taylor, 'Challenges to Building an Effective Asia-Pacific Security Architecture', in Michael J. Green and Bates Gill (eds), *Asia's New Multilateralism: Cooperation, Competition and the Search for Community* (New York: Columbia University Press, 2009), pp. 454–87; pp. 463–4.

4 On ASEAN generally, see Shaun Narine, *Explaining ASEAN: Regionalism in Southeast Asia* (Boulder, CO: Lynne Rienner, 2002).

5 See Michael Leifer, *The ASEAN Regional Forum*, Adelphi Paper, no. 302 (London: Oxford University Press, 1996).

6 ASEAN Secretariat, 'The ASEAN Regional Forum: A Concept Paper', http://www.aseanregionalforum.org/.

7 Akiko Fukushima, 'The ASEAN Regional Forum', in Michael Wesley (ed.) *The Regional Organizations of the Asia-Pacific: Exploring Institutional Change* (Basingstoke: Palgrave Macmillan, 2003), pp. 76–95, pp. 89–90.

8   See John Garofano, 'Power, Institutions and the ASEAN Regional Forum', *Asian Survey*, vol. 42, no. 3, 2002, pp. 502–21, pp. 512–4.

9   On its development and constraints, see Rodolfo C. Severino, *The ASEAN Regional Forum* (Singapore: ISEAS, 2009).

10 On America's attitude to the ARF, see Evelyn Goh, 'The ASEAN Regional Forum in United States East Asia Strategy', *The Pacific Review*, vol. 17, no. 1, March 2004, pp. 47–69.

11 'Singapore Declaration on the 15th ARF', ASEAN Regional Forum, 24 July 2008, http://www.aseanregionalforum. org/.

12 ASEAN Secretariat, *ASEAN Regional Forum Vision Statement* 23 Jul 2009, http://www.aseansec.org/Doc-ARF-Vision-Statement.pdf.

13 For the decision to hold the exercise, see 'Chairman's Statement 15th ARF', ASEAN Regional Forum, 24 July 2008, http://www.aseanregionalforum.org/.

14 See ARF/VDR website for details: http://www.pia.gov.ph/arfvdr/?m=1.

15 Jürgen Haacke, 'The ASEAN Regional Forum: from dialogue to practical security cooperation?', *Cambridge Review of International Affairs*, vol. 22, no. 3, 2009, pp. 429–48.

16 Iran, India, Mongolia and Myanmar have observer status. Belarus and Sri Lanka became dialogue partners in 2009.

17 'Declaration on the Establishment of the Shanghai Cooperation Organisation', 15 June 2001, http://www.sectsco.org/ EN/. Also found at http://en.sco2009. ru/docs/documents/declaration.html.

18 Kevin Sheives, 'China Turns West: Beijing's Contemporary Strategy towards Central Asia', *Pacific Affairs*, vol. 79, no. 2, 2006, pp. 205–24.

19 Marcel de Haas, *The 'Peace Mission 2007' Exercise: the Shanghai Cooperation Organization Advances*, Central Asian Series 07/28, Advanced Research and Assessment Group, Defence Academy of the United Kingdom, http://www.clingendael. nl/publications/2007/20070900_cscp_ paper_haas.pdf.

20 See generally Rollie Lal, *Central Asia and its Asian Neighbours: Security and Commerce at the Crossroads* (Santa Monica, CA: Rand Corporation, 2006).

21 'Declaration on the Establishment of the Shanghai Cooperation Organisation', 15 June 2001, http://www.sectsco.org/ EN/. Also found at http://en.sco2009. ru/docs/documents/declaration.html.

22 'Dushanbe Declaration of SCO Member States', 28 August 2008, http://www. sectsco.org/EN/show.asp?id=90.

23 'Yekaterinburg Declaration of the Heads of the SCO Member States', 16 June 2009, http://www.sectsco.org/EN/ show.asp?id=87.

24 Gene Germanovich, 'The Shanghai Cooperation Organization: A Threat to American Interests in Central Asia?', *China and Eurasia Forum Quarterly*, vol. 6, no. 1, 2008, pp. 19–38, pp. 23–7, http://www.isdp.eu/files/ publications/cefq/08/gg08scoamerica. pdf; and Michael Raith and Patrick Weldon, 'Energy Cooperation and the Shanghai Cooperation Organization: Much Ado about Nothing?' *EuroAsia Net Commentary*, 25 April 2008, http:// www.eurasianet.org/departments/ insight/articles/eav042508b.shtml.

25 See Nick Bisley, 'Securing the "Anchor of Regional Stability"? The Transformation of the US–Japan Security', *Contemporary Southeast Asia*, vol. 30, no. 1, 2008, pp. 73–98.

26 On the Trilateral Security Dialogue generally, see William T. Tow, Mark J. Thomson, Yoshinobu Yamamoto and Satu Limaye (eds), *Asia-Pacific Security: US, Australia and Japan and the New Security Triangle* (London: Routledge, 2007).

27 On this and the Trilateral Security Dialogue, see Nick Bisley, 'The Japan–Australia Security Declaration and the Changing Regional Setting: Wheels, Webs and beyond?', *Australian Journal of International Affairs*, vol. 62, no. 1, March 2008, pp. 38–52.

28 For example, see Hugh White, 'Tri-lateralism and Australia: Australia and the Trilateral Security Dialogue with America and Japan', William T. Tow et al (eds) *Asia-Pacific Security* (London: Routledge, 2008) pp. 101–111.

29 For typical examples, see 'Trilateral Strategic Dialogue: Joint Statement', 27 June 2008, http://www.foreignminister. gov.au/releases/2008/fa-s080627.html and 'Trilateral Strategic Dialogue: Joint Statement by the United States, Japan and Australia', 21 September 2009, http://www.foreignminister.gov.au/releases/2009/fa-s090921d.html.

30 William T. Tow, 'The Trilateral Strategic Dialogue: Facilitating Community Building or Revisiting Containment', National Bureau of Asian Research, in *The Trilateral Strategic Dialogue*, NBR Special Report No. 16, December 2008, pp. 1–10, http://www.nbr.org/publications/element.aspx?id=354.

31 'Japan-China-ROK Trilateral Summit, Joint Statement for Tripartite Partnership', 13 December 2008,, http://www.mofa.go.jp/region/asia-paci/jck/summit0812/partner.html.

32 'Joint Statement on the Tenth Anniversary of Trilateral Cooperation among the People's Republic of China, Japan and the Republic of Korea', 10 October 2009, http://www.mofa.go.jp/region/asia-paci/jck/meet0910/joint-1.pdf.

33 Donald E. Weatherbee, 'Three Minus ASEAN: The Dazaifu Summit', *PacNet*, No. 2, 8 January 2009, http://csis.org/publication/pacnet-2-january-8-2009-three-minus-asean-dazaifu-summit.

34 For the Zone of Peace, Freedom and Neutrality Declaration text, see: http://www.asean.org/3629.htm.

35 For the Treaty of Amity and Cooperation in Southeast Asia text, see: http://www.asean.org/1217.htm.

36 The initial intention was to establish the ASEAN Security Community by 2020, but at the Cebu Ministerial Meeting in January 2007 members decided to bring this forward by five years.

37 For the text of ASEAN Concord II see: http://www.asean.org/15159.htm.

38 ASEAN Secretariat, *ASEAN Political-Security Blueprint* (Jakarta: ASEAN Secretariat, 2009), http://www.aseansec.org/5187-18.pdf.

39 See Rudolfo C. Severino, 'Towards an ASEAN Security Community', ISEAS *Trends in Southeast Asia Series*, no. 8, 2004, http://www.iseas.edu.sg/82004.pdf.

40 The meetings have been in May 2006, November 2007 and March 2009.

41 'Joint Declaration of the ASEAN Defence Ministers on Enhancing Regional Peace and Stability', 14 November 2007, http://www.aseansec.org/21135.htm.

42 'Joint Declaration of the ASEAN Defence Ministers on Strengthening ASEAN Defence Establishments to Meet the Challenges of Non-Traditional Security Threats' 26 February 2009, http://www.aseansec.org/22314.pdf.

43 For example, Alan Collins, 'Forming a security community: lessons from ASEAN', *International Relations of the Asia-Pacific*, vol. 7, no. 2, 2007, pp. 203–35; pp. 218–9.

44 On APEC, see Richard E. Feinberg (ed.), *APEC as an Institution: Multilateral Governance in the Asia-Pacific* (Singapore: ISEAS, 2003).

45 John Ravenhill, 'From Poster Child to Orphan: the rise and demise of APEC', in Lorraine Elliott et al, *APEC 2007: The Search for Relevance,* Keynotes 07 (Canberra: Australian National University, Department of International Relations, Research School of Pacific and Asian Studies, 2007), pp. 4–15, http://rspas.anu.edu.au/ir/pubs/keynotes/documents/Keynotes-7.pdf.

46 On this generally see Malcolm Cook and Allen Gyngell, *How to Save APEC,* Lowy Policy Brief (Sydney: Lowy Institute for International Policy, 2005), http://www.lowyinstitute.org/Publication.asp?pid=305.

47 On the emergence of security cooperation at APEC, see Nick Bisley, 'APEC and Security Cooperation in the Asia-Pacific' in Anne Hammerstad (ed.), *People, States and Regions – Building a Collaborative Security Regime in Southern Africa* (Johannesburg: South African Institute of International Affairs, 2005), pp. 225–49.

48 See John Ravenhill, 'Mission Creep or Mission Impossible? APEC and Security', in Amitav Acharya and Evelyn Goh (eds) *Reassessing Security Cooperation in the Asia-Pacific* (Cambridge, MA: MIT Press, 2007), pp. 135–54.

49 See APEC, 'Sydney Leaders' Declaration on Climate Change, Energy Security and Clean Development', 9 September 2007, http:// www.apec.org/.

50 Richard Stubbs, 'ASEAN Plus Three: Emerging East Asian Regionalism?', *Asian Survey* vol. 42, no. 3, 2002, pp. 440–55.

51 Chu Shulong, 'The ASEAN Plus Three Process and East Asian Security Cooperation' in Amitav Acharya and Evelyn Goh (eds), *Reassessing Security Cooperation in the Asia-Pacific*, pp. 155–76.

52 See Wen Jiabao, 'Work Together to Build an East Asia of Peace, Prosperity and Harmony', 14 January 2007, http://www.fmprc.gov.cn/eng/wjdt/zyjh/t290180.htm.

53 'Joint Communiqué of the First ASEAN Plus Three Ministerial Meeting on Transnational Crime', 10 January 2004, http://www.asean.org/15645.htm. For the text of the most recent meeting see http://www.asean.org/21041.htm.

54 'Joint Statement of the ASEAN + 3 Health Ministers' on Severe Acute Respiratory Syndrome', 10–11 June 2003, http://www.asean.org/14823.htm.

55 See both the 'Chairman's Statement of the 11th ASEAN Plus Three Summit', 20 November 2007, http://www.asean.org/21096.htm, and the 'Chairman's Statement, 10th ASEAN Plus Three Foreign Ministers' Meeting', 22 July 2009, http://www.aseansec.org/PR-42AMM-Chairman-Statement-ASEAN+3.pdf.

56 ASEAN Secretariat, 'Kuala Lumpur Declaration on the East Asia Summit', 14 December 2005, http://www.asean.org/18098.htm.

57 See Malcolm Cook, 'The United States and the East Asia Summit: Finding a Proper Home', *Contemporary Southeast Asia,* vol. 30, no. 2, 2008, pp. 293–312.

58 *Final Report of the East Asia Study Group* Phnom Penh, November 2002, http://

www.mofa.go.jp/region/asia-paci/
asean/pmv0211/report.pdf.

59 See Mohan Malik, 'The East Asia
Summit', *Australian Journal of
International Affairs,* vol. 60, no. 2, 2006,
pp. 207–11.

60 According to a US State Department
official in an off-the-record convers-
ation with author, Sydney, May 2008.

61 Cook, 'The United States and the
East Asia Summit: Finding a Proper
Home', p. 306.

62 See A.R. Kemal et al., 'A Plan to
Strengthen Regional Trade Cooper-
ation in South Asia' in T.N. Srinivasn
(ed.), *Trade, Finance and Investment in
South Asia* (Delhi, India: Social Science
Press, 2006), pp. 239–319.

63 'Declaration of the Fourteenth
SAARC Summit', 4 April 2007, http://
www.saarc-sec.org/data/summit14/
ss14declaration.htm. See particularly
Article 10.

64 'Additional Protocol to the SAARC
Regional Convention on the
Suppression of Terrorism', 6 January
2004, see http://www.saarc-sec.org/
main.php?id=11&t=3.2.

65 See, for example, 'Partnership for
Our People', Declaration at the 15th
SAARC Summit, 3 August 2009, http://
www.saarc-sec.org/data/summit15/
summit15declaration.htm.

66 See Peter Van Ness, *The North Korean
Nuclear Crisis: Four Plus Two – An
Idea Whose Time has Come,* Keynotes
04, (Canberra: Australian National
University, Department of International Relations, Research School of
Pacific and Asian Studies, 2003), http://
rspas.anu.edu.au/ir/pubs/keynotes/
documents/Keynotes-4.pdf.

67 See 'Initial Actions for the
Implementation of the Joint Statement',
13 February 2007, http://www.mofa.

go.jp/region/asia-paci/n_korea/6party/
action0702.html.

68 John S. Park, 'Inside Multilateralism:
The Six Party Talks', *The Washington
Quarterly,* vol. 28, no. 4, 2005, pp. 75–91.

69 Damon Bristow, 'The Five Power
Defence Arrangements: Southeast
Asia's Unknown Regional Security
Organization', *Contemporary Southeast
Asia,* vol. 27, no. 1, 2005, pp. 1–20.

70 Dewi Anwar Fortuna, 'Resource
issues and ocean governance in Asia
Pacific: an Indonesian perspective', in
Contemporary Southeast Asia, vol. 28,
no. 3, 2006, pp. 466–89; p. 486.

71 US Department of State, 'Proliferation
Security Initiative Participants', 27
May 2009 http://www.state.gov/t/isn/
c27732.htm.

72 'The PSI Maritime Interdiction Exercise
Hosted by Japan', 18 October, 2004,
http://www.mofa.go.jp/POLICY/un/
disarmament/arms/psi/exercise-2.html.

73 These 11 allies were: Australia, France,
Germany, Italy, Japan, the Netherlands,
Poland, Portugal, Spain, and the United
Kingdom.

74 US Department of State, 'The
Proliferation Security Initiative:
Statement of Interdiction Principles',
4 September 2003, http://www.state.
gov/t/isn/c27726.htm.

75 See Mark J. Valencia, *The Proliferation
Security Initiative: Making Waves in
Asia,* Adelphi Paper 376, (London:
Routledge, 2005).

76 Desmond Ball, Anthony Milner and
Brendan Taylor, 'Track 2 Security
Dialogue in the Asia-Pacific: Reflections
and Future Directions', *Asian Survey,*
vol. 2, no. 3, 2006, pp. 174–188.

77 See Brian L. Job, 'Track 2 Diplomacy:
Ideational Contribution to the Evolving
Asian Security Order' in Muthiah
Alagappa (ed), *Asian Security Order:*

Instrumental and Normative Features (Stanford, CA: Stanford University Press, 2002), pp. 241–79

[78] Japan Center for International Exchange, 'Track II: Multisectoral Policy Meetings', *Dialogue and Research Monitor: Inventory of Multilateral Meetings on Asia Pacific Security and Community Building* http://www.jcie.or.jp/drm/2007/track2.html.

[79] See Job, 'Track 2 Diplomacy'.

[80] See generally, Roger Buckley, *The United States in the Asia-Pacific since 1945* (Cambridge: Cambridge University Press, 2002).

[81] Cited, for example, in Buckley, p. v.

[82] For a discussion of America's recent policy, see Victor D. Cha, 'Winning Asia', *Foreign Affairs*, vol. 86, no. 6, 2007, pp. 98–113. For a contrary view, see T.J. Pempel, 'How Bush Bungled Asia: militarism, economic indifference and unilateralism have weakened the United States across Asia', in *The Pacific Review*, vol. 21, no. 5, 2008, pp. 547–81.

[83] Countries with bilateral treaty relationships with the US: Australia, Japan, South Korea. Australia's relationship is governed by ANZUS, a trilateral treaty including New Zealand. However, NZ has suspended its participation due to differences over nuclear policy. As such, ANZUS is effectively a bilateral agreement. Those with quasi-alliance relationships include the Philippines, Taiwan, Thailand and Singapore.

[84] See the discussion on the comprehensive security concepts coming out of recent reviews of the use of force in the light of experiences in Afghanistan and Iraq, in Carl Baker and Brad Glosserman 'From kinetic to comprehensive: new thinking in the U.S. military', in *PacNet*, no. 57, 31 October 2008, http://csis.org/publication/pacnet-57-october-31-2008-kinetic-comprehensive.

[85] Robert G. Sutter, *China's Rise: Implications for US Leadership in Asia*, Policy Studies no. 21 (Washington DC: East West Center, 2006), http://www.eastwestcenter.org/fileadmin/stored/pdfs/PS021.pdf.

[86] Department of Foreign Affairs and Trade (Australia), 'Japan-Australia Joint Foreign and Defence Ministerial Consultations', 6 June 2007, http://www.foreignminister.gov.au/releases/2007/fa064_07.html.

[87] See generally, Emma Chanlett-Avery and Bruce Vaughn, 'Emerging Trends in the Security Architecture in Asia: Bilateral and Multilateral Ties Among the United States, Japan, Australia, and India', *Congressional Research Service*, 7 January 2008, http://opencrs.com/document/RL34312/.

[88] On this and future challenges, see Michael D. Swaine, 'Managing China as a Strategic Challenge' in Ashley Tellis, Mercy Kuo and Andrew Marble (eds), *Strategic Asia 2008-09: Challenges and Choices* (Seattle, WA: National Bureau of Asian Research, 2008), pp. 70–105.

[89] DFAT (Australia), 'Joint Press Conference with Chinese Foreign Minister', 5 February 2008, http://www.foreignminister.gov.au/transcripts/2008/080205_jpc.html.

[90] 'China, Japan to hold 8th strategic dialogue', 20 February 2008, http://english.gov.cn/2008-02/20/content_894736.htm.

[91] 'The Sixth Japan-Republic of Korea (ROK) Vice-Ministerial Strategic Dialogue', 2 June 2008, http://www.mofa.go.jp/announce/event/2008/6/1180613_936.html.

Chapter Three

1 On this, see Bill Emmott, *Rivals: How the Power Struggle Between China, India and Japan will Shape our Next Decade* (London: Allen Lane, 2008).

2 For example, David Martin Jones and Michael L.R. Smith, 'Making Process, not Progress: ASEAN and the Evolving East Asian Regional Order', *International Security*, vol. 32, no. 1 (Summer 2007), pp. 148–84.

3 For example, Alex Bellamy, *Security Communities and their Neighbours: Regional Fortresses or Global Integrators* (Basingstoke: Palgrave Macmillan, 2004).

4 See Nicholas J. Wheeler and Tim Dunne, 'East Timor and the new humanitarian interventionism', *International Affairs*, vol. 77, no. 4, 2001, pp. 805–27.

5 Mely Caballero-Anthony, 'SARS in Asia: Crisis, Vulnerabilities, and Regional Responses', *Asian Survey*, vol. 45, no. 3, May–June 2005, pp. 475–95.

6 These attempts include the ASEAN Regional Forum's *Singapore Declaration on the 15th ARF*, 24 July 2008, http://www.aseanregionalforum.org; and the ASEAN Secretariat's *ASEAN Regional Forum Vision Statement* 23 Jul 2009, http://www.aseansec.org/Doc-ARF-Vision-Statement.pdf.

7 Kevin Rudd, 'It's time to build an Asia Pacific Community', Address to the Asia Society Australasia Centre, Sydney, 4 June 2008, http://www.pm.gov.au/node/5763.

8 For a discussion of this, see Graeme Dobell, 'Asia Pacific Community: An Idea, an Envoy and a plan' *The Interpreter*, Lowy Institute for International Policy, 15 October 2008, http://www.lowyinterpreter.org/post/2008/10/15/Asia-Pacific-Community.aspx.

9 Brad Norington, 'Barack Obama's man Kurt Campbell junks Kevin Rudd's Asia-Pacific plan', *The Australian*, 12 June 2009, http://www.theaustralian.com.au/news/barack-obamas-man-kurt-campbell-junks-kevin-rudds-asia-pacific-plan/story-0-1225733580240.

10 John Ravenhill, 'APEC adrift: implications for economic regionalism in Asia and the Pacific', *Pacific Review*, vol. 13.no. 2, June 2000, pp. 319–33.

11 Robert Hartfiel and Brian L. Job, 'Raising the risks of war: defence spending trends and competitive arms processes in East Asia', *The Pacific Review*, vol. 20, no. 1, March 2007, pp.1–22.

12 See Allan Gyngell, 'Design Faults: The Asia-Pacific's Regional Architecture' *Lowy Institute Policy Brief* (Sydney: Lowy Institute for International Policy, 2007).

13 On this, see Anne O. Krueger, 'Are Preferential Trading Arrangements Trade-Liberalizing or Protectionist?', *Journal of Economic Perspectives*, vol. 13, no. 4, Fall 1999, pp. 105–24.

14 See Evan S. Medeiros, 'Strategic Hedging and the Future of Asia-Pacific Stability', *The Washington Quarterly*, vol. 29, no. 1, Winter 2005–06, pp. 145–67; particularly pp. 148–53.

15 IISS, 'Modes of Security Cooperation: Confidence Building, partnerships, alliances', Chapter Nine of *Shangri-La Dialogue Report 2008*, http://www.iiss.org/publications/conference-proceedings/shangri-la-dialogue-report-2008/plenary-session-6/.

16 For two different assessments of Asia's regional order, see Nick Bisley, 'Neither Empire nor Republic: American Power and Regional Order in the Asia-Pacific',

International Politics, vol. 43, no. 2, April 2006, pp. 197–218, esp., pp. 210–14; and Evelyn Goh, 'Great Powers and Hierarchical Order in Southeast Asia', *International Security,* vol. 32, no. 3, Winter 2007/08, pp. 113–57.

Chapter Four

1   See http://www.pm.gov.au/node/5763.
2   'Hatoyama pushes East Asian community' *Asahi Shimbun* 23 September, 2009, http://www.asahi.com/english/Herald-asahi/TKY200909230045.html.
3   See Allan Gyngell, 'Design Faults: The Asia-Pacific's Regional Architecture', *Lowy Institute Policy Brief* (Sydney: Lowy Institute for International Policy, 2007); and Jusuf Wanandi, 'ASEAN Charter and remodelling regional architecture', *Jakarta Post,* 3 November 2008.
4   For example, Samuel S. Kim (ed.), *The International Relations of Northeast Asia* (Lanham, MD; Rowman and Littlefield, 2004).
5   For example, Ian Bremmer, Choi Sung-hong and Yoriko Kawaguchi, 'A New Forum for Peace', *National Interest,* no. 82 (Winter 2005/2006), pp. 107–12; Francis Fukuyama, 'Re-envisioning Asia', *Foreign Affairs* vol. 84, no. 1, 2005, pp. 75–87.
6   'U.S. Hopes Six-Party Talks Can Be Model for Northeast Asia', Department of State, *Washington File* 2005, http://usinfo.org/wf-archive/2005/050818/epf404.htm.
7   Remarks in Joint Press Conference, Tokyo, 27 February 2008, http://2001-2009.state.gov/secretary/rm/2008/02/101384.htm.
8   Off-the-record remarks by a senior State department official, Shangri-La Dialogue, Singapore, May 2009.
9   For the text of that agreement see: 'Initial Actions for the Implementation of the Joint Statement', 13 February 2007, http://www.mofa.go.jp/region/asia-paci/n_korea/6party/action0702.html.
10   See, for example, 'Australia calls for Northeast Asia security structure', ABC Radio Australia, 2 April 2008, http://www.abc.net.au/ra/programguide/stories/200804/s2205827.htm.
11   Fukuyama, 'Re-envisioning Asia'.
12   Jonathan D. Pollack, 'The Korean Peninsula in US Strategy: Policy Issues for the Next President' in Ashley J. Tellis, Mercy Kuo and Andrew Marble (eds), *Strategic Asia 2008-09: Challenges and Choices* (Seattle, WA: National Bureau for Asian Research, 2008), pp. 135-64; p. 149.
13   The ADMM-Plus concept paper is found at http://www.aseansec.org/21216.pdf.
14   According to one Vietnamese diplomat talking off the record at the Asia Pacific community conference Sydney, 4 December 2009.
15   Shiv Shankar Menon, 'The Evolving Balance of Power in Asia', paper presented to *Global Strategic Review: The New Geopolitics,* 13 September 2009, http://www.iiss.org/conferences/global-strategic-review/global-strategic-review-2009/plenary-sessions-and-speeches-2009/fifth-plenary-session-shiv-shankar-menon/.

16 After using a capital 'C' in the initial address, subsequent references have pointedly used a lower-case 'c' to refer to the community in an effort to make the proposal appear less prescriptive.

17 Kevin Rudd, 'It's time to build an Asia Pacific Community', Address to the Asia Society Australasia Centre, Sydney, 4 June 2008, http://www.pm.gov.au/node/5763.

18 Kevin Rudd, 'Eighth IISS Asian Security Summit Keynote Address', 29 May 2009, http://www.iiss.org/conferences/the-shangri-la-dialogue/shangri-la-dialogue-2009/plenary-session-speeches-2009/opening-remarks-and-keynote-address/keynote-address-kevin-rudd/.

19 Richard Woolcott, 'Towards an Asia-Pacific community', http://www.lowyinterpreter.org/post/2009/11/02/APC-The-Woolcott-paper.aspx.

20 'Hatoyama pushes East Asian community', Asahi Shimbun 23 September 2009, http://www.asahi.com/english/Herald-asahi/TKY200909230045.html.

21 'Address by HE Dr Yukio Hatoyama, Prime Minister of Japan, At the Sixty-Fourth Session of the General Assembly of the United Nations', 24 September 2009, http://www.mofa.go.jp/policy/un/assembly2009/pm0924-2.html.

22 Peter Alford, 'Japan favours Australian inclusion in East Asia community', The Australian, 8 October 2009, http://www.theaustralian.news.com.au/story/0,25197,26179518-2703,00.html.

23 Ben Doherty, 'China Backs Asia forum plan' The Age, 26 October 2009, http://www.theage.com.au/national/china-backs-asia-forum-plan-20091025-hepy.html.

24 On the current trends in Japan's modernisation, see Christopher W. Hughes, Japan's Remilitarisation (London: Routledge, 2008).

25 C. Raja Mohan, 'India and the Balance of Power', Foreign Affairs, vol. 85, no.4, 2006, pp. 17–32.

26 Nick Bisley, 'The Japan–Australia security declaration and the changing regional security setting: wheels, webs and beyond?', Australian Journal of International Affairs, vol. 62, no.1, 2008, pp. 38–52

27 For an example of this institutional logic see G. John Ikenberry, 'The Rise of China and the Future of the West', Foreign Affairs, vol. 87, no. 1, (January/February 2008), pp. 23–37.

28 Richard K. Betts, 'The United States and Asia', in Tellis et al (eds), Strategic Asia, 2008-09, pp. 41–68, on p. 55.

29 Stephen Grenville and Mark Thirlwell, A G-20 Caucus for East Asia, Lowy Institute Policy Brief, October 2009, http://www.lowyinstitute.org/Publication.asp?pid=1153.

30 For discussion of this with regard to China, see Justin Hempson-Jones, 'The Evolution of China's Engagement with International Governmental Organizations: Toward a Liberal Foreign Policy?', Asian Survey, vol. 45, no. 5, 2005, pp. 702–721.

31 IISS, 'Towards a New Asian Security Architecture' in Strategic Survey 2009 (London: Routledge, 2009), pp. 64–74.

32 See, for example, Brad Norington, 'Barack Obama's man Kurt Campbell junks Kevin Rudd's Asia-Pacific plan', The Australian, 12 June 2009, http://www.theaustralian.com.au/news/barack-obamas-man-kurt-campbell-junks-kevin-rudds-asia-pacific-plan/story-0-1225733580240.

33 Varun Sahni, 'India and the Asian Security Architecture', Current History, April 2006, pp. 163–8.

Conclusion

[1] See, for example, Anne-Marie Slaughter, 'America's Edge: Power in the Networked Century', *Foreign Affairs*, Jan/Feb 2009, and Richard N. Haass, 'The Age of Nonpolarity – What Will Follow US Dominance' in *Foreign Affairs* May/Jun 2008.

[2] See Christopher Kinsey, *Corporate Soldiers and International Security: The Rise of Private Military Companies* (London: Routledge, 2006).

[3] Stephen Fidler and Arlen Harris, 'Pirates hold Malacca Strait shipping hostage to fortune' *The Financial Times*, 23 June 2005, p20.

[4] For details see Patrick J. Cullen, *Private Security in International Politics: Deconstructing the State's Monopoly of Security Governance* Unpublished PhD thesis, London School of Economics, May 2009, Chapter Six.

[5] Kishore Mahbubani, *The New Asian Hemisphere: The Irresistible Shift of Global Power to the East* (New York: Public Affairs, 2008).

Adelphi books are published eight times a year by Routledge Journals, an imprint of Taylor & Francis, 4 Park Square, Milton Park, Abingdon, Oxfordshire OX14 4RN, UK.

A subscription to the institution print edition, ISSN 0567-932X, includes free access for any number of concurrent users across a local area network to the online edition, ISSN 1478-5145.

2010 Annual Adelphi Subscription Rates		
Institution	£457	$803 USD
Individual	£230	$391 USD
Online only	£433	$763 USD

Dollar rates apply to subscribers in all countries except the UK and the Republic of Ireland where the pound sterling price applies. All subscriptions are payable in advance and all rates include postage. Journals are sent by air to the USA, Canada, Mexico, India, Japan and Australasia. Subscriptions are entered on an annual basis, i.e. January to December. Payment may be made by sterling cheque, dollar cheque, international money order, National Giro, or credit card (Amex, Visa, Mastercard).

For more information, visit our website: **http://www.informaworld.com/ adelphipapers.**

For a complete and up-to-date guide to Taylor & Francis journals and books publishing programmes, and details of advertising in our journals, visit our website: **http://www.informaworld.com.**

Ordering information:
USA/Canada: Taylor & Francis Inc., Journals Department, 325 Chestnut Street, 8th Floor, Philadelphia, PA 19106, USA. **UK/Europe/Rest of World:** Routledge Journals, T&F Customer Services, T&F Informa UK Ltd., Sheepen Place, Colchester, Essex, CO3 3LP, UK.

Advertising enquiries to:

USA/Canada: The Advertising Manager, Taylor & Francis Inc., 325 Chestnut Street, 8th Floor, Philadelphia, PA 19106, USA. Tel: +1 (800) 354 1420. Fax: +1 (215) 625 2940.

UK/Europe/Rest of World: The Advertising Manager, Routledge Journals, Taylor & Francis, 4 Park Square, Milton Park, Abingdon, Oxfordshire OX14 4RN, UK. Tel: +44 (0) 20 7017 6000. Fax: +44 (0) 20 7017 6336.

0567-932X(2009)49:5;1-W